Masterpieces of Glass

A WORLD HISTORY FROM THE CORNING MUSEUM OF GLASS

ROBERT J. CHARLESTON

Masterpieces of Glass

A WORLD HISTORY FROM THE CORNING MUSEUM OF GLASS

HARRY N. ABRAMS, INC., PUBLISHERS, NEW YORK

A CORNING MUSEUM OF GLASS MONOGRAPH

Frontispiece: detail of plate 34,
cristallo goblet with enameled
and gilt decoration

Project Editor: Robert Morton
Editor: Joan E. Fisher
Designer: Judith Michael

LIBRARY OF CONGRESS CATALOGING IN PUBLICATION DATA
Charleston, Robert J.
Masterpieces of glass from the Corning Museum of Glass.
Bibliography: p.
Includes index.
1. Glassware—History. 2. Corning, N. Y. Museum of Glass.
I. Corning, N. Y. Museum of Glass. II. Title.
NK5106.C47   748.2′9   79–17657
ISBN 0–8109–1753–X

Library of Congress Catalog Card Number: 79–17657

Printed and bound in Japan

Masterpieces of Glass

A WORLD HISTORY FROM THE CORNING MUSEUM OF GLASS

Foreword

It was the particular genius of Arthur A. Houghton, Jr., that conceived The Corning Museum of Glass. Faced with the approach of Corning Glass Works' hundredth birthday, he, his cousin Amory Houghton, then Chairman of the Board, and their colleagues within the corporation decided to celebrate by establishing and maintaining a glass center—a unique institution devoted to the history, art, and manufacture of this one material. The center opened on May 19, 1951; chartered by the Board of Regents of the State of New York, the museum shared space with the Hall of Science and Industry, the factory where Steuben glass was made, and various community and company facilities, including a thousand-seat combination auditorium-basketball court and ten bowling alleys.

The museum's original collection was particularly strong in English glass because Steuben Glass, Inc. (a division of Corning Glass Works) had acquired major pieces between 1942 and 1950. During this period an antique glass shop was located in the mezzanine of the New York store under the direction of Douglas Carson, whose acquisitions included the 1577 Verzelini Goblet, the Ravenscroft Goblet with seal, and the Pembroke Goblets enameled by the Beilbys. Before the museum opened, a group of ancient glasses was purchased from Fahim Kouchakji, and the great McKearin Collection of American blown glass was added. Most of the other major areas of glassmaking were represented in the original collection by pieces bought singly or in small groups on the New York market. One exception was the purchase from Nellie B. Hussey of Kansas City of seven hundred pieces of glass jewelry collected by her in Peking between the two world wars.

When the museum opened in 1951, there were 2,206 pieces in the collection. Now, thirty years later, The Corning Museum of Glass has moved into its own building with a collection so vast and so rich that it is unsurpassed anywhere in the world. The objects pictured and described in this volume are some of the most noteworthy. The areas they represent include thousands of other pieces covering many facets of glass history: the Smith and Sangiorgi collections of ancient glass, the Beinecke Collection

Verrerie en bois, l'operacion de tirer le Pot hors de l'Arche. From Denis Diderot, et. al. Encyclopédie ou dictionnaire raisonné des sciences, des arts, et des metiers, 1772

7

of German enameled glass, the McKearin Collection of American historical flasks, the Esterly Collection of pressed glass, the Houghton and Battson paperweight collections, and, most recently, that superb panorama of glass drinking vessels, the Strauss Collections. Augmenting these are three decades of one-by-one curatorial acquisitions made by purchase and gift—more thousands of pieces forming sub-collections in every conceivable area, from ninth- and tenth-century Islamic carving to contemporary whimsical sculpture from California.

This continuous process of rebuilding the history of glass—object by object—gives rise to two questions: How did pieces made of such a fragile material survive? And, what might have been made in the past of which there are as yet no known survivors? In terms of ancient glass the answer to the first is related largely to custom—for example, where glass vessels were used in burials, the archeologist's shovel and broom have turned up ancient pieces often intact and sometimes quite free of surface decomposition. In more recent times, esteem has probably saved more glasses than custom; the value people have placed on particular vessels because of their intricacy, or beauty, or symbolic function caused their successive owners to take special care. The Guild beaker (no. 37) bearing signatures dating from 1574 to 1706 is such a treasure. Then, of course, there are the accidents—the walled-up storage room, the shipwreck, even the fires, floods, and earthquakes that suddenly stopped the ordinary flow of events, burying all under the debris of catastrophe—as at Pompeii.

But the second question is the haunting one—what has *not* survived? Where are the ancient ceilings, walls, and floors of colored glass of which only small bits are known to us? Where are the glasses that custom decreed should be destroyed—such as toasting glasses—or objects so ordinary that no one saved any—like an ancient windowpane? A history built on evidence must reflect the peculiarities of survival, as does this one. But the collection grows, and with the arrival of each new piece comes new information and sometimes new questions.

With the commitment to establish the museum, the founding fathers put particular emphasis on the formation of the library. Important early manuscripts and incunabula representing such original sources as Pliny, Josephus, and Agricola went on exhibition with the opening of the building. Of more pragmatic value is the large research library developed and operated under a mandate to collect everything of any consequence whatsoever, regardless of language, on the art and history of glass and glassmaking. And so it has. Today, the library includes more than 20,000 volumes and is growing at the rate of 750 to 1,000 volumes a year. Bibliographies are published regularly and distributed to scholars and libraries throughout the world.

But the cornerstone of the museum's research activities is the *Journal of Glass Studies*. Published annually since 1959, it covers an extraordinary range of scholarly investigation—from Mesopotamian archeology to Bauhaus functionalism—a kind of ongoing international seminar spreading out over the years and including most of the major scholars active during the last quarter century. Prominent among these scholars from the very beginning has been Robert Charleston, formerly Keeper of Glass and Ceramics at London's Victoria and Albert Museum. His revelations have been presented regularly in the *Journal* and from the podium at the museum's annual Fall Collectors' Seminar, but as mentor and friend he has also counseled successive directors and curators of The Corning Museum in the formation and study of the collections. At this wonderful moment in the museum's evolution—with the opening of a new building and the presentation of the history of glass in unparalleled depth—Robert Charleston is the consummate guide. In the following pages he leads us through a forest of singular objects, the pick of the museum's first thirty years, the beginnings of whatever new growth is to come.

Thomas S. Buechner
Director, The Corning Museum of Glass
Corning, New York

Introduction

This book is an attempt to present the history of glass through the collections of The Corning Museum of Glass. Opened in 1951, the museum has acquired through gift and purchase nearly twenty thousand glasses from all periods, and displays one of the most comprehensive collections of glass in the world. Emphasis on scope alone, however, may be misleading. Throughout the period of its existence the museum has striven to acquire the finest examples of particular kinds of glass, and it has had a very large measure of success, obtaining many pieces from well-known collections, some of them world-famous in their own right. Among such glasses may be mentioned, for example, the Disch Kantharos (no. 20); the Daphne Vase from the R. W. Smith Collection (no. 15); the Populonia bottle (no. 19) among Roman glasses; the de Rothschild enameled *lattimo* bowl (no. 35); the Verzelini glasses, of which no. 39 here is one, among the glasses made in Venice or in the Venetian style; the earliest English lead crystal glasses, the Ravenscroft pieces, of which no. 63 is one; the Hans Wessler plaque, the only known work by this early Nuremberg engraver (no. 59); the Amelung covered beaker engraved with "Tobias and the Angel," unique among the incunabula of early American glassmaking (no. 84); the Fritsche Ewer, masterpiece of one of the greatest Bohemian engravers of the nineteenth century and a landmark for the American glass decorators of the 1870s and later (no. 91). All these are glasses of the utmost importance, but the history of glass cannot be built around such pieces alone. It has therefore been the aim to include in this volume typical, but not necessarily "important," glasses from the museum's collection which epitomize the virtues of a particular phase of glassmaking (nos. 17, 38, 44, 48, 64). Very often they are more beautiful than the "important" glasses, such as those listed above.

Some of the most important branches of the glass industry are necessarily excluded from the survey, since beer bottles and windowpanes seldom rank high on the aesthetic scale. It should not be forgotten, however, that these humble products were very often the backbone of the industry, providing an economic base for the production of more ambitious objects.

It is impossible to represent the whole of glass history by any group of a hundred glasses or by the collection of any single museum. If the attempt has to be made, however, Corning is the best place to make it. Only here, in a museum dedicated solely to glass, has a consistent and sustained policy been followed that aims to create a collection that not only includes masterpieces but also covers the whole history of the art, as far as is possible, from its earliest beginnings up to the present.

To understand this history, an effort of imagination is essential. To the primitive glassmaker, totally ignorant of chemistry, his art was a sort of magic that by fire converted the basest ingredients—dust and ashes—into a fragile, transparent, impenetrable, shining substance fit for adornment or the table. James Howell, the seventeenth-century Anglo-Welsh *littérateur* who knew the glass industry from the inside, put it well when he wrote of Venice: "The art of glass-making is here very highly valued, for whosoever be of that profession are gentlemen *ipso facto*, and it is not without reason, it being a rare kind of knowledge and chymistry to transmute dust and sand (for they are the only main ingredients) to such a diaphanous pellucid dainty body as you see a Crystal-Glass is. . . ." The workman who brought about this transubstantiation, however, although he might be a gentleman in name, sweated it out in front of the roaring heat of the glory hole for a longer working day than any modern legislation would tolerate; grew bad-tempered and threatened intruders with the hot end of his blowing iron; developed a great thirst, and gratified it.

Maurice Marinot, perhaps the greatest of modern glassmakers, who did not grow up

9

in the trade and therefore saw it with clearer eyes, summed up the *métier* of the glass-worker: "To be a glassman is to blow the transparent stuff close to the blinding furnace, by the breath of your lips and the tools of your craft, to work in the roasting heat and the smoke, your eyes full of tears, your hands dirtied with coal dust and scorched. It is to produce an order of simple lines in the sensitive material by means of a rhythm which matches the life of the glass itself, so that in due course you may rediscover in its gleaming stillness that life of the human breath which will evoke living beauties."

The craft demanded even more of its workers when a pot broke or wore out and had to be changed for a fresh one. The wall of the furnace was then broken down and the full force of the fire unleashed while the men struggled to remove the glowing pot with iron bars and levers. For this, the worst chore in the industry, they "cloath themselves with a Garment made of skins in shape of a Pantaloon, which they make as wet as possible and which covers them all over except the Eyes and for them they make use of Glass to see to guide themselves." So wrote a French author at the end of the seventeenth century. Nearly a hundred years later the great French *Encyclopédie* of Diderot and D'Alembert illustrates the scene, the workmen wearing long smocks and those nearest the pot with slouch hats pulled down over their ears and held in place with scarves. Such scenes are less common today, although scarcely less picturesque. Far more primitive modes of glassmaking, however, may still be seen in the East, where the gaffer (master glassblower) often works single-handed, with no more than a boy to help him keep the furnace fueled. He has no long-armed chair like the modern gaffer, but trundles his iron on his thigh just as the glassmaker must have done who is represented on the earliest-known illustration of glassmaking—the eleventh-century manuscript of Hrabanus Maurus in the monastic library of Monte Cassino. He sits on a three-legged stool, and this was the normal practice in Europe until well into the seventeenth century. Some of the most beautiful glasses ever made demanded no more equipment than these men used and still use.

Since scrutiny of the one hundred and two glasses selected has necessarily brought with it a certain partiality, it may be well here to sketch in the broader lines of glass history, to provide a context into which they may be fitted and to give depth and texture to the picture. Having cleared away any preconceptions gained by visiting a modern glasshouse or from other circumstances, we may imagine the glassmaker at his work, ill clad, in a hovel or a broken-down shed, busying himself about a furnace, probably no higher than himself, which is pouring out heat and some smoke by way of the hole through which he must withdraw the molten glass and return it for re-heating when it becomes too stiff to work. In the earliest days, it may be supposed that the glass was worked in a relatively pasty state, and the operation may have resembled that of a cook icing a cake rather than that of a modern glassmaker.

The earliest furnaces were not capable of high temperatures (in the mid-fourteenth century that at Tel el Amarna in Egypt, for example, probably did not reach 1100°, whereas in Renaissance Europe and later temperatures of about 1500° were normal). Glass vessels were formed on a core held on a metal rod and made of a sandy clay mixed probably with animal dung to give it cohesion and a certain elasticity. Onto this the glass was probably applied in threads by means of a metal rod, the half-finished vessel being reheated repeatedly and marvered (rolled) on a flat, smooth slab to consolidate the threads. When the body was formed, decorative threads of contrasting colors were applied in much the same way, then dragged with a point or comb to form festoon or feather patterns, perhaps in imitation of the markings in such natural stones as alabaster. Any further accessories, such as a button foot, spreading neck, or handles were then added and the vessel cooled. The metal rod was withdrawn and the core picked out.

Already at the earliest dates known to us, glass was made of varying colors, all opaque, and since at later dates colored glasses are known to have been traded in slabs and ingots for working up, it is believed that they were the product of specialized

Illuminated miniature from the manuscript of Hrabanus Maurus, "De Universo," datable to 1023 A.D. Abbey of Monte Cassino (Codex 132)

knowledge kept carefully secret in the glasshouse that could make them. It is important to realize that there is a distinct difference between the knowledge of how to make glass and how to work it. In the case of beads and bangles, for instance, only a small workshop would be necessary, with no more plant than bellows, crucibles, and a supply of canes of colored glass. The methods of working were probably not very different from those for the earliest vessels, and since small beads and amulets certainly preceded vessels in time, the core technique probably derived from that used earlier for making small, solid objects. Such an establishment could be set up wherever there was sufficient fuel and access to the required glasses. Fortunately, primitive equipment is no bar to artistry.

Had these glassworkers been the subjects of a survey, they would probably have been classified as metalworkers. Into quite a different category would have gone the second group of glassworkers known from early times. They treated glass in its quality of being a stone ("poured stone" is indeed one of the Greek expressions for glass), handling it in the same manner as they did semiprecious stones, by rubbing and grinding it with abrasives to reduce it to the required shape and size. These men were themselves probably stoneworkers and lapidaries, accustomed to carving and inscribing stones of a far more intractable hardness. At Tel Asmar in Mesopotamia, in buildings dating from the dynasty of Sargon of Akkad (c. 2500 B.C.), a lapidary's kit was found along with finished and half-finished stone seals and included a borer belonging to a bow drill. This primitive instrument continued in use for boring and grinding for four thousand years, and it is still used in workshops in the East. It is difficult for modern people to appreciate just how many hours of labor were expended in working intractable materials with such primitive tools.

The contrast between hot working and cold working is absolute, and until the end of the eighteenth century, cutting and engraving shops were quite separate from the glasshouses that supplied their blanks. Moreover, there has been a constant tug-of-war between these two styles of glass decoration, first one and then the other appealing to the taste of succeeding epochs.

Long before glass was drawn out into threads and manipulated in the ways already described, it had probably been molded into amulets and the like—a natural extension of metallurgical processes, the nearest analogies available to the earliest glassworkers. Once glass had been used for vessels, it would have been natural to carry the molding process into this field too, a development that seems to have occurred at least as early as the eighth century B.C. A further extension was the molding of patterned canes, produced by making the desired design in the cross section of a thick rod and then extending it so that the pattern shrank as the rod was pulled out. The attenuated rod could then be cut across and the sections placed side by side in a refractory mold and heated until deformed and run together into a single sheet of glass. It is not known exactly how the molding process was carried out, but during the first millennium B.C. and into the first century A.D. these techniques were refined and perfected in ways that baffle the modern mind.

The progress of this type of glassmanship, which might have seemed set to go on forever, was drastically altered about the middle of the first century B.C. by the invention of glassblowing. It has been suggested, and it seems logical in view of the earlier dominance of molding, that the vital discovery was made in the course of working on molding processes, and that the earliest blown glasses may have been those blown in a mold. Present evidence suggests, however, that glass was already being free blown by about 40 B.C. This liberating innovation revolutionized the production and use of glass, and it is probably true to say that glass was more widely used, for a greater variety of purposes, during the period of the Roman Empire than at any time subsequently until the sixteenth or seventeenth century. The wholesale production of glass for containers and windows was accompanied by a more limited range of decorative and luxury glasses, produced for the rich and the very rich, which has never been surpassed in elaboration of technique and perfection of craftsmanship. A great variety of colored glasses was used in the most complicated variations of the old molding techniques, sometimes with the addition of gold leaf, which was also used for gilt surface decoration and for "sandwiching" between two layers of glass married together.

It was perhaps in this area of the industry that the most astonishing effects were produced. Apart from the superficial decoration of vessels by facet cutting and even figural engraving of varying degrees of excellence, the Roman *diatretarii* (glass cutters) produced two types of glass that have not been surpassed in modern times. The first involved the cutting of layered glasses (again imitating hardstones) so that a design in one color stood in relief on a ground of another, the most famous in this genre being the Portland Vase (in the British Museum). The second technique involved the production of a decorative openwork skin undercut so as to stand free of the surface of the vessel except for a few supporting struts. When a vessel decorated with a figural subject cut in this way is itself made of a dichroic glass, which is greenish by reflected light but a rich wine-red by transmitted light, the summit of sophistication may be said to have been reached. Such combinations of craftsmanship and technology were not to be seen again for nearly two thousand years.

The colored glasses of the early Imperial period were gradually supplanted toward the end of the first century A.D. by the use of a colorless "crystal" material as the luxury glass *par excellence*. This was much used for cutting and engraving and also formed a base for painted decoration in enamel colors and gold.

Only the centralized power of Rome made possible such developments, and with the breakup of the empire much of the old cunning was lost. In northern Europe, glass continued to be made in a relatively rough, green unpurified material, decorated only with simple mold-blown designs or applied threading, mostly self-colored but occasionally in an opaque white, presumably imported from more civilized parts. In the East, however, the centers of culture in the Romanized lands bordering the Mediterranean, as well as those that had arisen in Sasanian Persia, were overrun in the course of the seventh century A.D. by Muhammad's fanatical followers, who poured out from the Arabian peninsula to conquer the world in the name of Islam. Despite the inherent iconoclastic tendencies of their religion, the Arabs gradually adopted the art forms practiced by the Christian Syrians and Copts and the Zoroastrian Iranians over whom they now ruled; among these was glass. Syrian glassmaking always had been renowned for its manipulative skills; the Persians had excelled in glass cutting and engraving. Both these fields of glass continued to be cultivated during the Umayyad and Abbasid caliphates, but with subtle adaptations of form that gave the glasses an unmistakable Islamic flavor. Distinctive Islamic technical contributions to the art were the use of pincers to apply a decorative motif or an inscription to the walls of an open vessel and the joining together of two parisons (or gathers of glass)—one of colorless, the other of colored glass—in a single vessel. Later, from the twelfth century onward, the old Roman art of enameled and gilt glass was revived with particular splendor, especially in Ayyubid and Mamluk Syria during the thirteenth and fourteenth centuries.

Far less is known of glassmaking in the neighboring Byzantine dominions, although a form of enameling and gilding on colored glasses seems to have been practiced there with great distinction. This fact, as well as the distinct Islamic look of the glasses made at Corinth, the only identified glassmaking center in Byzantine territory, suggests that there was a strong oriental influence on Byzantine glass, as there was on Byzantine textiles. The Corinth glasses, however, also have their affinities with glass farther west, and here Corinth was more probably the giver than the receiver. Many glasses found on medieval sites in Italy reveal traits common to the Corinth glasses, such as a virtually colorless material decorated with applied threads in blue, stemmed forms, characteristic beaker forms with flared lips, and an occasional vessel made in opaque red glass. A number of thirteenth- and fourteenth-century sites in northern Europe have turned up glasses that display one or more of the characteristics mentioned, and it can only be supposed that they were imported from Italy, where Venice in the next century was destined to bring this influence to a triumphant climax. The most striking fact is that a true colorless glass was widely current in Europe well before the middle of the fifteenth century, the date that by tradition has been ascribed to the "invention" of *cristallo* by Angelo Barovier in Venice.

Venice, favored by history in its location between East and West and heir to much of the Byzantine legacy when Constantinople fell to the Turks in 1453, also prospered by dint of its own great exertions in politics and war. In commerce, apart from the transit trade, its strongest card was probably its glass industry, exiled to the island of Murano since 1292 but firmly under the control of the aristocracy in Venice itself. In this esoteric milieu, from which glassmakers were forbidden to emigrate under threat of condign punishment, a great ferment of ideas carried glassmaking to hitherto undreamed-of heights in the second half of the fifteenth century. The old Islamic techniques of enameling and gilding, by now abandoned in the land of their birth, were revitalized and adapted. Colored glasses, and later *cristallo*, were gilt with gold leaf and then overpainted with colored enamels (of which the Venetians themselves had the secrets), at first in relatively heavily enameled figural scenes, then in lighter schemes of decoration with coats-of-arms and formal borders of etched gold-leaf and enamel dots.

With these glasses the Venetians took the Near East and Europe by storm, even supplying the mosques of Cairo with the lamps that their own artists had ceased to manufacture. The rage for enameled glasses seems to have abated during the second quarter of the sixteenth century, although not before the technique had been transplanted to France and central Europe, where it continued to be cultivated without a break long after Venice had abandoned it. In Venice its place was taken by *cristallo* decorated with incorporated threads of opaque white glass, whether plain or twisted into cables, forming striped patterns that emphasized the elegant profiles of the glasses they embellished. Other decorative devices that owe their origins to Venice at this period include the use of the diamond point to produce thin, scratched lines in designs commensurate with the skill of the artist, and "ice-glass," in which the hot parison was dipped in water, the resultant fissuring and roughness of texture being smoothed off on the marver. It might be argued, however, that the greatest Venetian contribution to glassmaking during this period was the production in their limpid crystal glass of the three-piece drinking glass (bowl, stem, and foot) in a wonderful variety of classic shapes requiring no further embellishment.

Despite the savage penalties exacted by the Venetian State, many Venetian glassmakers absconded from Murano in the sixteenth century to take their art into central and northern Europe; the concept of Venetian crystal, worked thin and fine, dominated European glassmaking throughout the sixteenth and until the mid-seventeenth century. The fine, simple forms, however, became progressively modified with ornament, and complex wrought decorations "of extraordinary fashions" became the vogue. In the third quarter of the seventeenth century, reaction set in and a different level of taste became apparent. In England and Germany experimentation led to the creation of a new type of glass—more solid and completely colorless in contrast to the always slightly brown- or gray-tinted Venetian material. George Ravenscroft, who by 1676 had perfected his recipe by using increasing quantities of lead oxide, referred in his application for a patent to "a particuler sort of Christaline glass resembling Rock Chrystall"; and in Germany, where a robust colorless glass was produced by the addition of lime, a work of 1679 refers to glass that "in transparency and brilliance came near to crystal." This production of a glass as nearly as possible resembling rock crystal was of particular significance in Germany and Bohemia, where wheel engraving was becoming an increasingly important means of decorating glass.

The whirligig of taste had turned again in favor of the stony aspect of glass, and in central Europe engraved glass (with or without cutting) was the preferred luxury product of the eighteenth century, much admired in the rest of Europe. In England the development took a slightly different course, the early years of the century being devoted to the evolution of a style of wrought glass in simple forms suitable to the slow-working, light-refracting properties of lead crystal. Before the middle of the century, however, glass cutting had established itself as a decorative technique uniquely suited to bringing out the hidden fire in lead glass. By the end of the eighteenth century English cut-glass was perhaps the most sought-after glass in the world. This dominance lasted well into the next century.

The popularity of crystal glass had reached the end of its allotted span by the middle of the nineteenth century. Turning its attention from engraving on colorless glass, the Bohemian industry developed a whole series of colored glasses, whether opaque in imitation of basalt and red marble or transparent for coating crystal glass in the "cased" technique, whereby cutting and wheel engraving were used to produce designs cut through to the underlying crystal and contrasting with the colored ground. Bohemia had an almost inexhaustible reservoir of skilled engravers and cutters, and they not only applied their skills to faceting, notching, and engraving the heavy profiled forms of this Biedermeier period in their own country but provided a steady stream of skilled men to work abroad. Bohemian glass dominated this era as English glass had the preceding half-century, and its styles were taken up and imitated in many European countries and in America.

The primitive glassmaker has by now been left far behind, and at this stage almost all the techniques available to the decorator of glass have been evolved, with two major exceptions. One is the use of mold pressing, which found its greatest development in the U.S.A. from the second quarter of the nineteenth century onward; the second is the use of acid etching (by means of hydrofluoric acid). The former made possible the cheap mass production of elaborately ornamented objects; the latter enabled the work of the engraver and cutter to be greatly abridged—acid ate away what had previously been removed by abrasion. It is scarcely necessary to give a sketch of the modern period here. With the invention of surface iridescence, all the technical resources were available to enable the artists of the Art Nouveau movement to realize their vision. Virtually no additional techniques have been developed in the twentieth century; one style has succeeded another, culminating in the work of individual artists in the modern studio movement.

Of the glasses themselves illustrated in this book, not all may appeal immediately to the reader as "masterpieces." Some knowledge is a useful prerequisite of fuller appreciation. Although the perceptive eye can sometimes see the quality of an object which the taste of the age rejects, this perception is usually the result of more training than is often suspected. The painter or draftsman is always looking at things; the average person virtually never uses his eyes critically. The abnormal experience of the artist when faced with an object can in some measure be replaced by knowledge of another sort. If we know the purpose for which an object was made, this knowledge is an aid—or in some cases a bar—to its appreciation, as one example may make clear. A European lady resident in Hong Kong, passing through the bazaar, noticed a pot of what seemed exceptional elegance; she bought it, and on her return home used it to hold a flower arrangement destined for her dinner table. At the sight of it her Chinese butler threw the thing out of the window, for to him it was a chamber pot and a disgrace to his household. Such prejudices have to be taken into account. Other useful forms of knowledge include an idea of the limitations imposed by the level of technical progress at a given moment in history. The kind of glass made in England in the eighteenth century (which seemed revolutionary to contemporary continentals) would have been impossible without the discovery of lead crystal toward the end of the seventeenth. In the notes that accompany the illustrations an attempt has been made to sketch such details of social, artistic, or technical context that may help the reader to a greater appreciation of the objects in this book.

Plates and Commentaries

1

Core-formed Egyptian Vase

The earliest glass objects so far known date from the middle of the third millennium B.C., at the earliest, and have all been found in western Asia (Mesopotamia, Syria, etc.). These are all small, solid objects such as beads, rods, and so forth; the earliest vessels from the same general area are dated on archeological grounds no earlier than the end of the sixteenth or the early fifteenth century B.C. It was about this time that the powerful pharaoh of Egypt, Tuthmosis III (1490–c. 1437 B.C.) of the Eighteenth Dynasty, was embarking on a policy of expansion to the northeast, pushing into Syria and up to the borders of Mesopotamia. The earliest datable glasses found in Egypt come from this time, three of them actually bearing the pharaoh's name in hieroglyphs. It is difficult to resist the conclusion that the Egyptians learned the art of making glass from this contact with western Asia.

The amphoriskos illustrated on the opposite page probably dates from the reigns of Tuthmosis's successors Amenophis III (c. 1401–1363 B.C.) or Amenophis IV (c. 1363–1346 B.C.), but it is made in the strong colors that characterize the earliest as well as the later Eighteenth Dynasty glasses—turquoise blue, dark blue, yellow, and white.

The glasses of this era were made on a core fixed to a metal rod, traces of the core often appearing on the inner surface of a vessel. The core seems to have been made of a mixture of a ferruginous clay and an organic material, probably dung, and often coated with a thin, white outer layer of limewash. The core, which was given the internal shape of the desired vessel, was covered with glass either by dipping into a crucible containing the molten material, or by trailing threads over the surface until it was covered. This was then smoothed by using a flat tool or by rolling the glass on a flat surface, probably made of stone. Threads of contrasting colors were trailed around the vessel in a spiral and dragged upward or downward, or both, to give feather patterns. The foot was separately applied, and the rim of the neck and edge of the foot were then trimmed with a thread of dark blue glass, while composite colored cables, made by twisting together threads of different colors, were laid around the junction of the neck with the body and of the body with the foot. At some point after the application of the decorative threads on the body, small vertical yellow handles were applied, part of one being visible in the photograph. When the glass was completed, the rod was withdrawn and the remains of the core were picked out.

Eighteenth Dynasty,
c. 1400–1350 B.C.
Height: 10.7 cm

2

Pharoah's Head in Cast and Retouched Glass

Glass had been used first in the Near East for the making of small objects such as beads, amulets, etc., when the factitious material presumably took the place of a semiprecious stone of comparable appearance. The development of glassmaking technique led on the one hand to the making of glass vessels (no. 1), and on the other to the production of larger glass objects, which were treated as if they were stone. A striking instance of this is the headrest of Tutankhamen, famous pharaoh of the later Eighteenth Dynasty (c. 1346–1337 B.C.). The headrest is made from two solid pieces of glass joined together, the join being covered by a gold fillet. The length of this object is slightly less than eleven inches; the height seven and a quarter inches. It is reasonable to presume that the two separate T-sections comprising the headrest were roughly cast to shape before being reduced by abrasion to their finished condition. The same process was no doubt used for the portrait head of one of Tutankhamen's predecessors, illustrated here.

This head has been tentatively identified as that of Amenophis II, son of the great Tuthmosis III, during whose reign the craft of glassmaking was probably first introduced into Egypt. A few portraits of Amenophis II are known in stone and are consistent with this likeness in glass. Moreover, the reign of Amenophis II was the first from which portrait sculpture in glass is known. Indeed, the earliest glass sculpture hitherto identified is a shawabti (a figurine represented as a mummy and intended to act as the deputy of the dead in the afterworld) belonging to no less a person than one Ken-amun, chief steward of Amenophis II himself. The head of the king is sensitively modeled and immaculately finished, the retouching and polishing probably having been carried out by means of the simplest tools and a great deal of hard work. The once blue glass is now heavily weathered, but the quality of the original surface has probably been preserved. The pharaoh is wearing the *nemes* headdress, which is meticulously rendered with incised lines, and the customary false beard. At the front of the headdress there was originally a *uraeus*, or cobra poised to strike, the serpent form of Edjo, of the tutelary goddess of lower Egypt.

The only close parallel to this piece is the head fragment of a king represented as a sphinx, also considered to be of the mid-Eighteenth Dynasty, in the British Museum in London; here, however, part of the shoulders survives. A number of royal portrait heads in glass are known, but they were designed to form parts of composite figures made up in other materials, such as glazed quartz fritware (faience), wood, ivory, gold, etc. In such cases, the back of the head is cut away to accommodate the bulky headdress in another substance, and the beard is missing, revealing the holes intended for its attachment. Even the eye sockets are normally empty. The completeness of the Corning head, therefore, suggests that it was part of a wholly glass portrait figure, perhaps of the king kneeling or depicted as a sphinx, rather than of such a composite figure.

Eighteenth Dynasty,
c. 1435–1415 B.C.
Height: 4 cm

3

Alabastron with Threaded Decoration

The glass industry which had reached its peak in Egypt with the vessels of the Eighteenth Dynasty (no. 1), and which also flourished in other parts of western Asia, went into a decline at the end of the thirteenth century B.C., with the general breakdown of Bronze Age culture in the Near East and the eastern Mediterranean. It certainly did not altogether die out, for not only are a few scattered objects known from both Iran and Egypt that date from before the renaissance of the art in the ninth century B.C., but the survival of similar techniques from the earlier to the later period seems to guarantee that there was some continuity of tradition.

The alabastron illustrated here reveals traits in common with the earlier period: it is core formed and decorated with an applied spiral of thread around the body and with individual threads around the orifice and just above the foot. A faint wavy effect has been given by drawing a pointed implement in vertical lines on the body, but without producing the pronounced arcade or feather patterns exemplified by the earlier Egyptian amphoriskos. The material used seems to lack the brilliance and solidity of the Egyptian glass and gives the impression of being more pasty in the working, an impression perhaps heightened by the way in which the glass weathers, producing an opaque gray color that obscures the original tint of the glass. The brilliance of the Egyptian glasses of the Eighteenth Dynasty and later is certainly in part due to the favorable conditions afforded by the dry soil of Egypt. The eyelet handles on this alabastron look forward to those of the comparable containers of the sixth century B.C. and later made probably in the eastern Mediterranean. The name alabastron itself is of Greek derivation, meaning an alabaster container for ointment, and is something of a misnomer in a ninth-century B.C. context. It does, however, point to the use for which these small vessels were destined as containers for unguents or perfumes. Glass vessels of any kind were of the greatest rarity at this early period, and they were naturally used for the preservation or transport of comparably precious substances.

Probably Mesopotamian,
8th–7th century B.C.
Height: 16.8 cm

4

Late Hellenistic Amphoriskos

The method of making small vessels on a removable core continued until the invention of glassblowing, probably toward the end of the first century B.C., and probably overlapped with the newer process in some places for a time. The old core-forming technique, which had flourished in the second millennium B.C. in Egypt and the Near East, continued into the first millennium in Mesopotamia and Syria (not in Egypt) and thrived particularly in the eastern Mediterranean from the sixth century B.C. onward. The centers of production were probably on the Syrian coast itself, and possibly also in Rhodes and Cyprus. The objects they produced had a wide distribution not only in the Mediterranean but also as far afield as south Russia on the one hand and Gaul (modern France) on the other. Whether the Phoenicians made the vessels or not, it seems likely that they played a large part in their distribution by way of trade.

From the sixth century B.C. onward these small vessels, used for the transport and storage of precious perfumes, tended to follow the shapes of Greek pottery—the tubular alabastron, innumerable variants of the two-handled amphora (amphoriskos), the globular aryballos with short neck and ring handles, and miniature versions of the wine jug, or oenochoe.

The amphoriskos shown here mimics in its applied button base the pointed finial of many Hellenistic amphoras. Its decoration consists of a single spiral of applied thread that has been drawn by a point into an arcade design covering the central area of the body.

Eastern Mediterranean, probably 1st century B.C. Height: 24 cm

24

5

Cast and Cut Vase

The Greeks had two separate expressions for the word "glass," one roughly translatable as "poured stone" and probably to be equated with the furnace-worked vessels of the type of nos. 1, 3, 4. The other word, *hyalos,* carried overtones of clarity that are hardly applicable to the glasses referred to. This epithet could justly be applied to a category of glasses of great antiquity, dating to the eighth century B.C. at latest. These are usually solid vessels of greenish glass that have obviously been worked over by abrasive methods—that is, by grinding the surface with some substance harder than the glass itself, probably by means of fast-turning wheels. The lug handles of the vase illustrated have been drilled vertically, perhaps for the attachment of a cover, and the most famous of this family of glasses—the Sargon Vase in the British Museum—shows signs of internal grinding by rotary tools. Since these vessels have been abraded outside, and in the case of the closed shapes, internally too, it is clearly very difficult to decide just how the original form was made—whether the vessel was ground from a solid block of glass or whether a roughly shaped blank was first cast and then reduced by abrasion.

The earliest of this family of glasses is a bowl from Gordion (now in modern Turkey) dating from the eighth century B.C. (no. 6), and there is a series of less elaborate bowls of a similar glass material found in Mesopotamia and the Mediterranean area that seem to range in date from as early as the late eighth to the sixth century B.C. More closely comparable with the Corning vase, however, is a class of vessels of closed shapes, including the Sargon Vase, datable by a cuneiform inscription engraved on it referring to the Assyrian king of that name (Sargon II, reigned 722–705 B.C.). This was found in Nimrud, capital of the Assyrian Empire, and from the same source came a more squat "vase" with comparable neck and lug handles, presumably of the same date. The lug handles are found again in a series of slim alabastra (no. 3) found in Italy, Cyprus, and Syria, and probably of a slightly later date than the Nimrud objects. If they were made in the Near East, as seems most likely from the Gordion and Assyrian evidence (literally hundreds of comparable fragments have been found at Nimrud), their distribution indicates that they must have been articles of trade. This probability is confirmed by three more objects: the shape of one is very like the Corning vase, found at Praeneste (Italy); the second is a beautiful two-handled vase found in Bologna in a context indicating a date before 525 B.C.; the third, a fragmentary ewer found in Spain. This last piece is particularly important because it echoes in shape ewers of the eighth to sixth centuries B.C., in both metal and pottery, which are peculiar to the Phoenicians. In addition, it has a cartouche (in this resembling the Sargon Vase) enclosing a garbled hieroglyphic inscription such as might have been composed by one familiar with, but not expert in, the Egyptian language. The Corning vase itself was acquired in Egypt. It seems, therefore, extremely likely that these pieces were transported by the Phoenicians, the greatest trading nation of the time, throughout the Mediterranean area. Moreover, since the ewer is specifically Punic in shape and was found in Punic territory (Spain), it seems most probable that the Phoenicians made and traded these transparent greenish glasses.

*Mesopotamian or Syrian,
probably 7th-6th century* B.C.
Height: 19.2 cm

27

6

Cast and Cut Glass Bowl

The technique of building a vessel on a core was less suitable for making objects of an open shape, such as bowls and dishes, and a second Near Eastern tradition differed markedly in its technical approach. Not only was the glass material made as clear and colorless as possible, but the resultant vessels were intended to be finished by abrasion. In most cases this was probably done by the use of fast-turning wheels fed with powder from stones such as corundum. Closed shapes such as vases, jugs, and alabastra were also made of this transparent greenish glass and were drilled out internally as well as shaped and polished externally by means of rotary abrasion. Pieces of this kind date from as early as the eighth century B.C. and continue probably as late as the sixth century, but they are exceptionally rare.

Far commoner are dishes and shallow bowls. The earliest piece of this kind is a fragmentary dish found at Gordion in the territory of the ancient kingdom of Phrygia, datable to about the end of the eighth century B.C. This was decorated with a central raised boss corresponding to a concavity on the outer surface, and with thirty-two radiating round-tipped petals worked in relief on both sides of the glass, those on the outside appearing to be merely molded, those on the inside probably both molded and finished on the wheel. The molding was possibly achieved by letting powdered or finely fragmented glass melt down into a two-piece mold of refractory clay left within the furnace until the glass had flowed into all the interstices of the mold. The shape is one derived from contemporary metalwork, and the Gordion bowl is the earliest known in a long series where glass and metal bowls and dishes were made in parallel shapes. The dish illustrated has its petal decoration and central raised boss in common with the Gordion bowl, but differs from it in that the inside of the dish is plain. In its complete form, as in the Gordion example and many pieces in silver, the "mesomphalic" bowl could be firmly gripped by placing two fingers inside the boss and the thumb on the rim. In Aristophanes' play *The Acharnians* (425 B.C.), the Greek ambassadors to the Persian Court relate how "being guests we perforce drank the undiluted sweet wine from clear glass vessels and gold plate"; and almost colorless glass bowls have in fact been excavated at the Iranian capital city of Persepolis.

West Persian or Mesopotamian, probably 5th century B.C. Diameter: 17.5 cm

7

Hellenistic Cut Bowl

The fashion for drinking vessels of transparent, colorless glass, usually with a greenish tinge, which was evident in the eighth to fifth centuries B.C. in Persia and elsewhere in the Near East (no. 6), did not die out in subsequent centuries, although shapes and forms of embellishment underwent subtle changes. In the case of the bowl illustrated here, the petal motifs radiating from a central roundel, found on the earlier examples of the same form, have been varied so that the petals alternate with groups of three longer strokes that run right up to the horizontal cuts delimiting the upper edge of the decorated zone. Spaced evenly between these alternating motifs are twelve "fins" in high relief. A number of variants of this general form exist.

A comparable bowl from Canosa, in southern Italy and now in the British Museum, was found in company with a number of Hellenistic glasses of the highest quality which have confidently been dated to the third century B.C. This bowl, of greenish colorless glass, was decorated with twelve overlapping petals elaborately rendered and radiating from a central rosette, while twenty almond-shaped fins surround the bowl above the tips of the petals. At the other extreme of date, however, is a brown bowl decorated with sixteen long petals alternating with sixteen fins, found on a shipwreck off the little island of Antikythera, between Crete and the Greek mainland. This wreck has been dated about 80–50 B.C. but it is possible that the bowl was already of some age before it was loaded on board. This was a period when works of art from Greece were being shipped to Rome in quantity, "antiques" among them.

There is no evidence, however, that there was any significant glass manufacturing center in Greece at this period, although numerous Hellenistic cut glass bowls of other types have been found in Athens. Many of these are decorated with the same vertical fluting as may be seen alternating with the petals on the bowl shown here. With the establishment of the Greek Ptolemaic dynasty on the throne of Egypt (323 B.C.), Alexandria appears to have become an important center of glassmaking, and glassmakers from farther east probably migrated there with their skills. The luxurious "gold sandwich" glasses were probably an Alexandrian specialty in the Hellenistic period. They have many affinities with the clear, cut glass bowls, and examples were found along with the cut glasses at Canosa: all are likely to have come from Alexandria. Of the finned cut glass bowls, two further examples are known from Canosa and another from Xanthos in Lycia (Asia Minor), while a comparable bell-shaped cup with eight fins was found on the Attic island of Aegina. This shape has a close parallel in a silver example from the Aegean island of Ithaca that has been dated to the end of the third century B.C. This general distribution seems perfectly compatible with an origin in Alexandria.

Eastern Mediterranean,
perhaps Alexandria;
3rd–2nd century B.C.
Diameter: 17 cm

31

8

Mosaic Glass Plaque

The art of making mosaic glass had already been developed in Mesopotamia by the second half of the second millennium B.C. It consisted of fusing into a rod elements that together made a design in the cross section. When the rod was then heated and extended, the pattern remained unchanged except that it was continuously reduced in size as the rod was pulled outward. The earliest mosaic glasses were made by juxtaposing cross sections of single-colored rods in patterns, but already by about 1400 B.C. mosaic rods of concentric bands of different colors were being produced. By the Ptolemaic period in Egypt (323 to 30 B.C., when Rome finally took over the country), patterns of great complexity were made, as the Corning example here shows. Some repeat designs were made by juxtaposing sections from a single rectangular rod in a symmetrical arrangement, as was probably done with the design at the bottom of this plaque.

The Corning plaque shows an Apis bull, the manifestation in animal form of the Egyptian supreme god Osiris. The center of Apis worship was at Memphis, where solemn rites of great complexity were enacted whenever the bull of the moment died. These ceremonies involved embalming and transporting the heavy corpse to its final resting place, a considerable distance away, in the Serapeum at Saqqara. At the death of the old Apis, a new Apis was born, and after the obsequies the search began to identify by certain signs the bull calf that was the new embodiment of the god, in order that he might be installed in the place of his predecessor. The Greek historian Herodotus says that "Apis was a young black bull . . . on its forehead a white triangular spot," a blaze which can be clearly seen on the plaque. Between his horns the bull has a uraeus symbol, the cobra poised to strike. The uraeus represents the goddess Buto, tutelary deity of lower Egypt. It is shown here, as often in dynastic art, on the sun-disc between the horns of Apis.

The Ptolemies, despite their Egyptian and Greek origins, became enthusiastic supporters of the Apis cult, and contributed openhandedly to the expenses of successive funerals. The Apis bull, as the name suggests, was associated with the god Serapis, whose cult Ptolemy I had introduced as a state religion, aimed at uniting Egyptian and Greek. Although remaining independent of Serapis, Apis was nevertheless worshiped at the Alexandrian Serapeum, albeit in a separate shrine.

The Apis figure may therefore be seen as an eminently natural choice to be the theme of a decorative plaque—probably intended for the inlay decoration of a wall or piece of furniture—made in the great capital city of Alexandria, which we know from literary sources was also an important glassmaking center. It should be kept in mind that the illustration enlarges this plaque several times.

Egyptian, probably Alexandria;
1st century B.C. or A.D.
Height: 2.5 cm

32

9

Cameo Glass Cup

A constant theme running through early glassmaking is its emulation of hardstones, particularly rock crystal in clear, colorless glass, and the layered stones such as onyx and agate, imitated in the molded bowls of the first century B.C.–A.D. These layered hardstones, apart from being worked on the lathe into bowls and cups, etc., were also carved by the glyptic artists into "cameos." The stones were so prepared as to present an opaque white layer through which the artist carved down to the underlying colored layer (usually brown), thereby leaving his decoration both in relief and in contrasting color. The process was transferred to glass at some date not later than the Hellenistic era (323–30 B.C.). A plaque with a purely Egyptian subject exists which is considered to be of Ptolemaic date, and this early piece also suggests that the origin of this technique was in Alexandria (no. 7). It was probably later transplanted to Italy. Using this technique for a vessel was far more complicated than for a plaque, since the parison of the base glass (usually dark blue, but sometimes green-blue or blackish purple) had to be either "flashed" (dipped into a crucible of the opaque white glass), or "cased" (blown into a preformed open "bowl" of opaque white glass). In either case, it was essential that the two glasses be compatible in their rates of expansion and contraction; otherwise, cracks would develop on cooling, as the nineteenth-century imitators of the Portland Vase discovered to their cost (no. 92). That flashing was used rather than casing seems indicated by the fact that one fragment at Corning has no fewer than six layers of different-colored glasses. Once annealed (gradually cooled), the object was handed over to the cameo carvers—presumably the heirs of the hardstone carvers—to complete. Nothing is directly known of their equipment (no. 5), but it seems possible that, as in the nineteenth century, wheel engraving was supplemented by the use of burinlike tools and files. The true refinement of the art was to cut the opaque white layer so thin in places that the blue ground partially showed through, producing tonal as well as purely sculptural effects.

The shape of the Corning bowl is echoed in both pottery and metalwork, where the shape is familiar in the late Hellenistic period. It is also found in the molded glasses of the preblowing era and in representations on other cameo glasses of the same family. A number of whole, or completely reconstructible, cameo vessels survive, as well as a great many fragments. Most seem to portray Bacchic or Dionysiac scenes, sometimes of a mystical character. The theme of the Corning glass has been interpreted as a ritual in which a matron makes offerings to Silenus, companion of Dionysus, while two girls assist with the mystical ceremonies, one accompanied by a satyr. At the extreme end of the scene, the lady's riding mule is tethered to a tree.

Roman, perhaps Alexandria;
1st century B.C.
Height: 6.2 cm.
Gift of Arthur A. Houghton, Jr.

The bowl is said to have been found at Herakleia in Pontus (on the south coast of the Black Sea, in modern Turkey). It passed in due course into the collection of J. Pierpont Morgan, and is in consequence often referred to as the Morgan Cup.

10

Gold-band Pyxis

Pyxis was a Greek word originally denoting a container made of boxwood. The name was soon transposed to include boxes made in other materials, notably metal and pottery, and is normally used to describe a covered, cylindrical receptacle for ointments or medicines. It was ideally suited for the dressing table, a role it has continued to fill to the present day.

Expensive toiletries have always been put in expensive containers, but few of these can equal the luxurious complexity of the "gold-band" glasses of the early days of the Roman Empire. The same technique was used also to make alabastra for liquid perfumes and unguents that no doubt complemented the solid ointments or creams more likely to have been stored in the pyxides.

These vessels were not blown, but were laboriously constructed of bands of differing colored glasses, one element in them always being a ribbon of translucent glass in which embedded gold leaf had been "shattered" by expansion. The extraordinary care with which these glasses were made may be seen in the fact that colored glasses were often doubled with colorless glass to increase their translucency, these ribbons being sometimes as much as four layers thick. The bands were then fused together into sinuous patterns, and individual units comprising these patterns were laid side by side in a mold of the desired shape where they were fused together. Three such units compose the body and the lid of the example here.

On completion of this process, both parts of the pyxis were lathe-turned in order to correct any irregularities, to cut a ledge as a seating for the cover, and to finish the finial on the cover itself. For good measure, horizontal lines were cut as decoration below the cover recess and above the foot, as were two concentric grooves on the underside of the flat foot; similar lines decorate the lid.

The pyxis was acquired in Lebanon and probably reflects the extraordinary wealth and sophistication of the Hellenized Near East on the threshold of the Roman Imperial period.

Roman, perhaps Alexandria;
c. 50 B.C.–A.D. 25.
Height: 5.2 cm

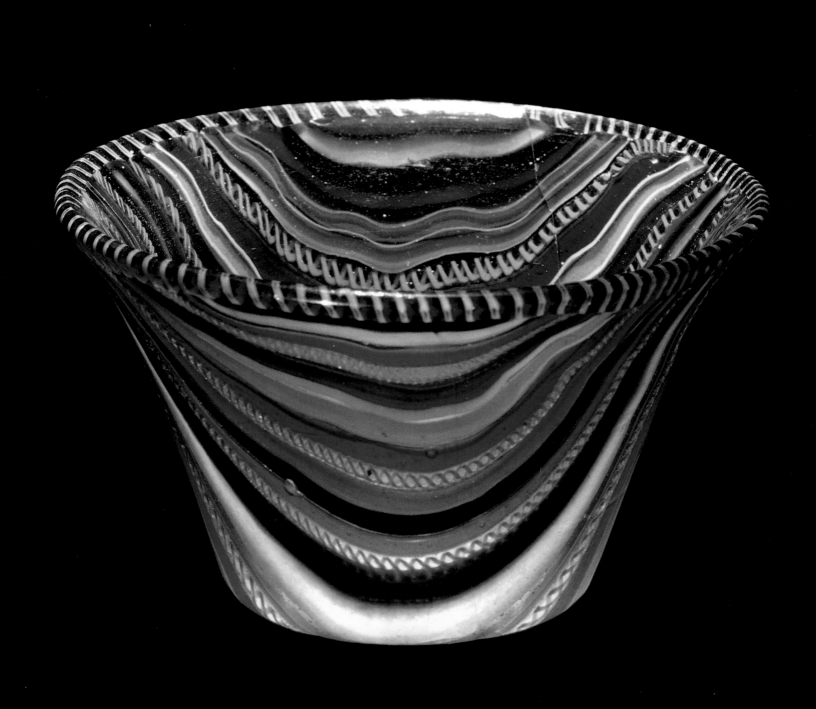

11

Ribbon Glass Polychrome Bowl

This bowl, of a shape rare in glass although with some parallels in pottery, illustrates the extraordinary complexity of ancient glassmaking techniques before the invention of glassblowing. Not only had the glassmakers of this period the necessary technological knowledge to produce the ten or so different transparent and opaque colors used in the making of this bowl, but they had already mastered the art (probably evolved as early as the third century B.C.) of making cables of glass by picking up two opaque white canes on opposite sides of a thicker rod of transparent glass, embodying them in this by marvering (rolling on a smooth surface), and finally drawing them out and twisting at the same time, to produce the cable effect (nos. 40, 41). They also possessed an extraordinary technical skill in disposing these canes in molding techniques that appear to be varied according to the requirements of the type of glass in hand (no. 10). As they were probably executed in a number of stages, and the traces of how they were done has often been obliterated by subsequent grinding, only speculation is possible. Here it would appear that the various canes had been fused in a pre-arranged sequence into three identical units which were then slowly heated until they sagged in the furnace over a convex fireproof clay mold. The resultant roughly shaped glass skin may then have been trimmed by shearing away the surplus glass at the edge and subsequently further molded by fusion in an external mold turned the other way up, the final bowl being trimmed around its inevitably irregular rim by means of a cable of blue glass spirally wound with white. Lastly, the whole bowl was ground by rotary means both inside and out, to get rid of any surface irregularities, and then polished.

Wall paintings from the Roman Imperial period in Italy and actual tomb finds both of glass vessels and those in other precious materials make it clear that drinking vessels were normally made in pairs. The Emperor Nero (37–68 A.D.) paid six thousand sesterces for "two moderate-sized drinking-cups, which they called Petro-ti" (perhaps a well-known type of goblet with wing handles); and Suetonius records of the same emperor, when he heard his fall was imminent, "He upset the table and dashed to the floor two favorite scyphi which he called 'Homeric' from the Homeric tales carved on them." The implication is that they were smashed, and since they were also carved, they must have been of either glass or crystal. It seems clear, however, that these cups went in pairs, and there is in the museum at Adria, in Italy, a second bowl exactly like the Corning example. It is tempting to surmise that originally they may have belonged together.

Roman, perhaps Italy;
1st century B.C. or A.D.
Diameter: 8.7 cm

39

12

Pillar-molded Bowl

Bowls, and shallower dishes, of the kind shown here are among the commonest luxury glasses found (usually in fragments) on Roman sites of the early and mid-first century A.D. Some of the earlier examples are in variegated "mosaic" and "millefiori" glasses of the general type represented here by no. 11. They are the obvious descendants of the Hellenistic bowls such as no 7. The technique of their production, however, was different, and although the details of how they were made are uncertain and many theories have been put forward, it seems evident that they were made in ribbed molds. Whether this was achieved by pressing or by slow melting of glass in the form of powder or small fragments, it is not clear, partly because the traces of how the bowls were made have been removed by subsequent grinding and polishing on the wheel.

This process is universally visible on bowls of this kind, both on and below the rim on the outside, where very often (as here) even the tops of the ribs have been shaved off instead of being left rounded as they came from the mold. The inside surface of the bowl is also normally entirely abraded. The ribs themselves, however, seem to have been given a "fire polish" at the "glory hole" of the furnace, and it is possibly during this process that some of them were occasionally distorted and had to be corrected by hand tools. In addition to the external and internal grinding and polishing, horizontal decorative lines were also incised on the inside of the bowl, a virtually universal form of decoration on the molded shapes of this phase of glass-making. The first-century writer Pliny referred to all this abrasive work in his brief sketch of the history of glassmaking in his *Natural History* (completed about 73 A.D.) when he wrote, "other [glass] is ground on a lathe" (*aliud torno teritur*).

With the political stability brought to the countries of the Near East by the establishment of the Roman Empire, freedom of movement had become practicable for craftsmen of all kinds, and glassmakers, probably from Alexandria, brought the molding processes to Italy well before the turn of the Christian era.

The Corning thirty-one-ribbed bowl is a masterpiece of its kind, of exceptional size and beautiful color.

Roman, probably Italy;
mid-1st century.
Diameter: 19.8–20 cm.
Gift of Mrs. Joseph de F. Junkin

13

Ewer of Mold-blown Glass

With the "Roman Peace" brought by the final domination of the Roman possessions by the Emperor Augustus, there was a mood of economic optimism and expansion and unprecedented freedom of movement within the empire. The tremendous wealth of Rome itself, and of Italy generally, attracted the luxury industries, and the expanding trade of Italy gave industry there a central position of great influence and profit. This centripetal tendency may be seen in the ceramic industry, where the Arezzo potteries suddenly blossomed about 30 B.C., using both techniques and workers of oriental origin. The same forces appear to have influenced the glass industry, and this development coincided with the revolution brought about by the invention of glass-blowing (no. 14).

The handsome mold-blown ewer illustrated opposite is inscribed under the handle in Greek: "Ennion made [me]." Another of identical design, but blue in color, is in the Haaretz Museum in Tel Aviv, and a third is in the Metropolitan Museum of Art in New York. This last piece, however, not only has a different handle, but terminates below at the horizontal line visible at the bottom of the body, resting on a flat base. A two-handled vase in the Hermitage Museum, Leningrad, and a hexagonal amphorisk in the Metropolitan Museum both come from different molds but have the same inscription and flat base. The New York ewer came from Istanbul, and the amphorisk from Cyprus, while the Leningrad amphora came from Kerch (Crimea)—a distribution that suggests an eastern Mediterranean origin. Two signed handleless bowls from Sidon, in Syria, strengthen this supposition. There is, however, a whole series—some fifteen—of handled cups with Ennion's mark found predominantly in north Italy, and therefore probably made there.

This evidence suggests that Ennion was a Syrian glassblower who either migrated to Italy or opened a branch there. That he was indeed from east of the Mediterranean seems likely not only because he signed in Greek, but because other "signed" mold-blown glasses—by Jason, Meges, and Neikaios—have been found exclusively in the Near East. All these makers included the formula "Let the buyer remember [me]" in their molds, and this appears on some of Ennion's glasses, too. All must have belonged to the same tradition. Other glassmakers' signatures establish that they were actually Sidonians—Neikon, Ariston, and Artas—but these seem so far to be known only on handles of vessels, the bodies of which have unfortunately disappeared. Almost all come from Rome, and a fragmentary bottle inscribed "Eirenaius of Sidon made [me]" was also found there. These Sidonians had evidently already migrated to Rome or its vicinity.

Pliny in his *Natural History* describes Sidon as "mastermaker of glass," but in another passage he refers to "Sidon once renowned for these [glass] workshops." This seems to suggest that Syrian glassmaking was then being overtaken by the Italian; the migrant Sidonians who proclaimed their origin on their wares may in fact have been trading on their past reputation.

The Ennion glasses are the most elegant of all the mold-blown glasses—with clear and well-drawn ornaments sharply reproduced in the new technique. Much credit should obviously accrue to the moldmaker.

The foot of the Corning glass has been restored according to the ewer in Tel Aviv.

*Roman, probably Syria
but perhaps Italy;
early 1st century.
Height: 23.5 cm*

14

Two-handled Vase in Dappled Glass

Most of the glasses so far discussed were made by forming on a core or casting in molds. The revolutionary discovery that changed the industry, and ultimately made glass available to everybody, was the invention of glassblowing. The discovery was so epoch making that it is perhaps surprising to find no specific mention of it in contemporary literature. Controversy has marked the subject ever since people became interested in the history of glass. With further archeological discoveries, however, it has become increasingly evident that this vital invention took place at some time in the third quarter of the first century B.C. Two separate finds in the territory of present-day Israel suggest that blown vessels were being made by about 40 B.C., and finds from a number of Italian sites of late Republican or early Augustan date (that is, about 35 B.C. onward) lead us to believe that blown glass was becoming available in Italy about the same time.

The writer Strabo states in his *Geography* (probably completed by about 19 A.D.) that at Rome "It is reported that there have been many inventions for producing various colors, and for facilitating the manufacture [of glass], as for example in glassware, where a glass bowl or drinking cup may be purchased for a copper coin." Strabo's actual words do not imply that he was aware of the nature of glassblowing, and the first specific mention of the process does not in fact occur in Latin literature until after the middle of the first century A.D. Both Strabo and, later, Pliny refer to the Phoenician coast, and particularly Sidon, as an important center of glassmaking, and these references, as well as the priority in date of the finds of blown glass in this general area, make it seem likely that the crucial invention was in fact made here (no. 13). It seems certain, however, that the process was speedily taken up in Italy, where the industry probably soon overtook its Eastern mentors and rivals.

The colorful amphorisk shown opposite was found in Syria. It is made of a transparent blue base glass that has been rolled on a marver strewn with chips of opaque glass—blue, white, red, and yellow. These have been expanded or elongated by subsequent blowing and working, to produce the texture of blobs and patches which characterizes this type of glass. Vessels of this general kind, often of blue glass but also of amber or purple, and with many varieties and combinations of colored decoration, have been found in archeological excavations in northern Europe, in contexts suggesting dates in the second or third quarter of the first century A.D.—as, for example, at Vindonissa and in the Tessin, in Switzerland; at Weisenau, in Germany; and perhaps as far afield as Colchester, in Britain. Other pieces, however, bearing a strong resemblance to the mold-blown glasses of Ennion (no. 13), have been found in south Russia, and thus point strongly to an origin in Syria. A handle from a two-handled drinking cup (scyphus) in this technique bears the mark, in both Greek and Latin, of the glassmaker Artas, who adds the word "Sidonius" ("a man of Sidon"). Artas belonged to the same glassmaking tradition as Ennion, but the finding of this fragment in Europe, as well as the appearance of Artas's signature in both Greek and Latin, point to an Italian origin. By the middle of the first century the Sidonian glassmen, who had probably started their activity in the vicinity of Rome, appear already to have moved into northern Italy—the Po valley and Aquileia—to be nearer the expanding markets of the northern provinces—Gaul, Germany, and Britain.

Roman, probably Syria; first half of 1st century. Height: 11.7 cm

15

Enameled and Gilt Opaque White Ewer

Enameling on glass has in modern times been effected by mixing in an oily medium powdered glass of a melting temperature lower than that of the glass to be decorated. This mixture (usually based on oil of lavender) can then be painted on the surface of the glass and permanently fixed by raising the temperature to the point when the medium is burned off and the "enamel" melts without causing the base glass to collapse. Enamels for painting on glass are usually opaque, and often in history it has been found advisable to use them on an opaque base glass (nos. 35 and 72). Until the eighteenth century, gilding was usually applied in the form of gold leaf or powder, and was fired separately, usually after the application of the enamels. It seems likely that Roman methods were similar.

The Daphne Vase was allegedly found in a concealed niche in a burial chamber at Kerch, in the Crimea, probably some time before 1905. Much Roman glass found in this area appears to be of Near Eastern origin, and Syria is indicated here by the fact that a closely comparable fragment—painted in the same way on an opaque white glass—was found in the excavations of the famous caravan city of Dura-Europos, on the Euphrates River in eastern Syria. Dura-Europos was destroyed by the Sasanian Persians, who drove the Romans out in 256 A.D., so the glass must have been made some time before this event. The Dura glass shows a female head with the remains of an inscription "Thet[i]s," and the vessel to which it belonged presumably depicted the myth of the fair-haired sea nymph Thetis, daughter of the sea god Nereus and mother of the hero Achilles. The scene represented was perhaps some event in the life of Achilles, or the marriage of Thetis with Peleus, where Eris (the goddess of discord) threw into the midst of the company the golden apple which was ultimately to be the cause of the Trojan War.

The decoration on the Daphne Vase also represents a myth. Daphne was also the daughter of a river-god, who is shown under the handle of the ewer, seated on a rock, and holding his conch horn, with his name "LADON" written above in Greek letters. To one side of him is the god Phoebus-Apollo (designated "PHOIBOS" in Greek characters), with his quiver of arrows, driven on by Cupid ("POTHOS") and in pursuit of Daphne, whom Cupid had filled with an aversion equaled only by Apollo's love. In response to her prayers the gods turned her into a laurel bush as Apollo reached her. It is this moment that is depicted on the ewer, showing Daphne half-tree, half-nymph. Around the neck of the ewer runs the inscription "Grace" ("CHARIS" in Greek).

Enameled glass was produced in Roman times in a number of centers other than Syria—probably in Egypt, in Italy in the first century A.D., and also later on in the northern glasshouses such as Cologne, probably in the third and fourth centuries.

Roman, probably Syria but perhaps Antioch; late 2nd or early 3rd century.
Height: 22.2 cm

16

Snake-thread Beaker

Over a hundred years ago the attention of those interested in ancient glass was drawn to a piece in the famous collection of Felix Slade (now in the British Museum), which was decorated in a distinctive way with applied ribbons laid on in angular and curved designs. The ribbons, of varying width, had been flattened against the surface of the vessel, apparently with a serrated tool that left diagonal hatching lines on them. With the publication in 1908 of Anton Kisa's foundation work on the history of ancient glass, it became general knowledge that a great deal of this glass was to be found in Germany, particularly Cologne, and as early as 1899 Kisa had coined the eloquent word *Schlangenfadengläser*, later translated into English literally as "snake-thread glasses."

It was for long assumed that these idiosyncratic vessels were a preserve of the Cologne glasshouses, but with the growth of the literature on ancient glass in the 1920s and 1930s, finds of comparable glasses from sites in the Near East came to light, and this body of evidence has grown greatly since World War II. In particular, glasses with "snake threads" of the same-colored glass, often supplemented by the figures of birds and sometimes of animals, have been found in some numbers in Cyprus, south Russia, the Syro-Palestinian area, and even farther east, the excavations at Dura-Europos contributing no less than seventeen fragments of this type. It is noteworthy that many of these eastern snake threads are impressed with a tool producing a waffle pattern rather than merely hatching. Colored threading is far less common, although examples have turned up in Egypt, Syria, and Greece.

These shifting patterns of distribution indicate that the technique most likely originated in the eastern parts of the Roman Empire in the first half of the second century A.D., with Syria specializing in same-colored trailing often with waffle-pattern markings. Eastern glassmakers expert in this type of manipulation then migrated either directly to Cologne, where glasshouses are known to have been at work by 50 A.D., or possibly via Italy (where a few fragments have been found). This east-to-west movement is discernible in a number of other branches of the industry (no. 13). In Germany these artists developed the coloristic side of the work beyond anything known in the East, employing opaque blue, yellow, sealing-wax red, and white glass for trailed designs of great complexity, sometimes supplementing or even replacing these with untooled, finer threading (sometimes gilt) in the form of coils, wreaths, ivy leaves, etc. The Corning beaker opposite represents a simpler form of this general style of decoration, which is nonetheless effective for its simplicity.

Roman, probably
Cologne, Germany;
3rd century.
Height: 11.5 cm

17
Ewer with Threaded Decoration

Rhenish,
3rd century.
Height: 28 cm

The complex decorative techniques invented or developed in Roman times have been illustrated in the preceding plates. It should be remembered, however, that the Roman Imperial period was unique in the extent to which glassmaking, stimulated by the enormous potentiality of glassblowing for mass production, was developed to meet every sort of domestic need. This occurred in both the eastern and the western provinces. Not only was glass made for all the purposes to which it had been put in the past, but it was manufactured in forms and for uses that had previously been the preserve of pottery and metalwork. Plain bottles of considerable size, square for ease of packing, were used for the transport of oil; they anticipated by nearly two thousand years some of the essential ideas of modern industrial design. Only their flattened handles were decorated, by means of vertical ribbing, which earns them the name of "celery handles."

Apart from the manifold uses of glass for the service of the table, small unguent flasks were made in enormous numbers and in a wide range of forms and sizes; window glass was largely used. All these types of practical objects were most frequently made without decoration in greenish or yellowish, unpurified glass. They are nevertheless often of great aesthetic attraction. The ewer illustrated has been chosen to represent the virtues of Roman glassmaking where the glassmaker relied on nothing but blowing and simple manipulation for his decorative effects. The tall and elegant, but yet stable, biconical form has been emphasized by the vertical applied threading on the body and by the emphatic tall handle; it is decorated in the way already alluded to and drawn upward from its solid point of application in a taut tapering line suddenly terminated by the right-angle turn at the top, and finished off by the characteristic looped embellishments. The broad rim is made by a complex double fold that not only gives it an appearance of solidity but in fact endows it with considerable strength, a fold being far more resistant to breakage and chipping than a single thickness of glass. The affinity between the disc of the foot and the disc of the rim helps to create the harmonious proportions that are characteristic of this type of jug, found in both the eastern and the western parts of the empire. The present jug may be judged on grounds of its material to be a product of the glasshouses in the Rhineland area of Germany, where Cologne in particular is known to have been a very important center of glassmaking (no. 16).

18

Wheel-engraved Bowl

There are essentially two methods by which designs can be incised on glass: one is by using a point of a harder material than the glass itself, scratching lines on it; the other is by using a swiftly rotating wheel onto which is fed a powdered abrasive. It is the abrasive that really cuts into the glass. Both these methods were used in Roman times. It cannot be said that much work of quality was done with the hardstone point, although it was sometimes effectively used in conjunction with wheel-cut facets to emphasize by curved hatching the three-dimensional nature of the form rendered. The true art of intaglio engraving, however, is essentially a sculptural one: to produce by the juxtaposition of concave facets a rounded three-dimensional effect. To this end a variety of wheels may be used—of different sizes and with different edge-profiles, either rounded, flat, or beveled.

Since no actual Roman engraving equipment has been preserved, and no contemporary description survives, only speculation is possible. However, it may reasonably be concluded, since the needs are essentially the same, that the glass engraver adopted the tools of the gem engraver, whose art stretches back unbroken into the second millennium B.C. There is evidence to show that the Hellenistic gem engraver used a cutting head driven by a bow lathe—that is, by a cord that takes a turn around the spindle of the lathe and is attached at both ends to a curved piece of wood. By pushing the bow backward and forward, a swift rotary movement is imparted to the spindle. This method has continued in use in the East for all sorts of industrial purposes up to the present and was described in use specifically for seal cutting in Persia in the seventeenth century, by which date in Europe a treadle-driven apparatus was normal. Often the bow was worked by a boy. We may suppose that the Roman wheel engravers, too, used some such apparatus.

We know that already by the first century B.C. glass was being lathe-turned, and that superb relief carving was being produced (no. 9). Intaglio engraving, however, probably came to the fore with the gradual dominance of colorless over colored glass toward 100 A.D. A number of the glasses already referred to, combining engraving with scratching, are dated to the second century; although this style is not unattractive, the engraver's true comprehension of three-dimensional form is missing, the defect being glossed over by the scratched detail. The best of third-century engraving is better, but this, too, tends to degenerate into a stylization all too evident in the fourth century, when every form is rendered by thin straight outlines and all texture by hatching. The eye on a face is a slit and the features are mere notches, a crew cut being the obligatory hairstyle. The centers of this glass-engraving industry appear to have been Egypt, perhaps Italy, and the Rhineland. This third- to fourth-century period also brought a widespread use of crude point-engraving in the north; and a style of superficial wheel engraving whereby the wheel just grazes the surface (no. 19, probably an Italian piece). Perhaps the more talented artists were drawn off into the prestigious workshops producing the ambitious undercut relief-decorated cage cups.

The tiny green bowl illustrated here is unusual, although by no means unique, in being decorated with a Christian subject—Christ and the Paralytic. The engraving, although showing some of the characteristics referred to, shows some comprehension of three-dimensional form.

Roman,
3rd–4th century.
Diameter: 6.3 cm

19

Wheel-engraved
Souvenir Bottle

Most of the bottles of this shape, with spherical body and a neck that tapers toward the rim and is pinched in above the body, come from German finds. At least eight whole flasks and fragments of two more bear wheel-engraved decoration that records the appearance of harbors on the Bay of Naples. These have been found in places as far apart as Britain in the north, North Africa in the south, and Portugal in the west. Four of them, however, were found in Italy, and there can be little doubt that they were made—certainly that they were engraved—in Italy itself, and probably at Puteoli (modern Pozzuoli). Views of Puteoli are represented on five of the known examples; within the boundaries of the city was a *clivus vitriarius*, or "hill of the glassmakers."

It used to be thought that all these glasses showed views of Puteoli, but it has recently been demonstrated that three of them, including the Corning flask, have instead views of Baiae, a neighboring resort on the promontory between Cumae and Puteoli. Although many features are common to both groups of bottles, whether showing Baiae or Puteoli (seaside towns tend to have features in common), the two known examples that correspond to the Corning flask include in their inscription the name "Baiae," and certain features of the view are specific to that place.

The Populonia bottle illustrated here is inscribed, "ANIMA.FELIX.VIVAS.," which may be roughly translated, "Long life to you, happy soul." Below this, or lower on the body, are the words, "STAGNV.PALATIV.OSTRIARIA.RIPA.PILAE" or "The pool. The palace. The oyster-beds. The shore. The pillars." each word being written over or close to the feature represented. The "Stagnu[m]" is undoubtedly an artificial lake constructed by the Emperor Nero. Suetonius writes, "Nero also undertook to build a pool stretching from Misenum to Lake Avernus, covered by a roof and enclosed by porticoes, into which he intended to turn all the hot springs which existed throughout the whole of Baiae." On one of the flasks the inscription indeed reads, "STAGNV.NERONIS" or "Nero's Pool." The palace (PALATIUM) was perhaps built by the Emperor Alexander Severus (222–235 A.D.) for his mother. As for the oyster beds, oysters were a favored dish among the Romans, and were brought from as far afield as Britain to be fattened in the Lucrine Lake, situated near Baiae on the Campanian Coast, and famous for this delicacy. Juvenal, writing at the end of the first century A.D., records that the true gourmet could distinguish by their flavor the oysters that came from Rutupiae (Richborough, on the Kent coast).

The bottles of this little family are distinguished by the common characteristic of being engraved very lightly, the glass being only touched on the wheel and moved across it in such a way that the engraver, as it were, drew his motifs on the glass rather than composing them from juxtaposed facets of varying shapes. The Corning bottle shows in addition sharply cut linear inscriptions with neat serifs and occasional fine details in the rendering of the scenes themselves. More than one engraver seems to have been employed on these glasses, and it may be surmised that they were popular souvenirs of a seaside vacation and were made in considerable numbers, just like the nineteenth-century Central European glasses engraved with views of Baden and other spas.

Roman, probably Puteoli, Italy;
late 3rd or 4th century.
Height: 18.4 cm

20

Gold-decorated Goblet
with Protective Network

This famous glass, usually known after a previous owner as the Disch Kantharos (kantharos denoting a vessel of this shape, originally in pottery), was probably excavated in Cologne in 1866 during road building. Its construction shows a close relationship with other glasses of the same date found in the same region. Noteworthy are the shape of the foot and the formation of the handles, which consist of pressed cockleshells joined together by threadwork. This motif recurs on some of the glasses of snake-thread type (no. 16), and on a beaker recently excavated in Cologne that is decorated entirely with vertical bands of such shell forms alternating with handles formed of thick, intertwined threads. These decorative elements form an openwork cage around the beaker comparable with that on the Corning glass. This feature tempts the thought that these glasses were the glassblower's answer to the cage cups of the glass cutter—magnificent vessels entirely covered with an open network of ornament cut from the substance of the glass and undercut to stand in full relief, free of the vessel except for an occasional supporting strut. This cut work, being enormously time-consuming, must have been costly in the extreme, and the furnace-worked goblets would presumably have offered an acceptable cheaper substitute.

The mesh ornament of the kantharos, however, serves also a practical purpose. It protects a zone of gilt decoration covering the bowl beneath. This shows winged *putti* (cupids) amid flowering plants below a plain band border.

A second goblet closely comparable with the Corning glass exists in Poland and came from the Czartorysky Collection at the Castle of Goluchow. Like the Corning glass, this, too, appears to have come to light in Cologne during road work at much the same time. It may reasonably be supposed that glasses of this general family were a specialty of one of the Cologne glasshouses, if not that which was responsible for the snake-thread glasses. Both the Corning and the Goluchow goblets have broken rims which probably originally projected higher above the level of the network.

Roman, Cologne, Germany;
probably 4th century.
Height: 13.5 cm

56

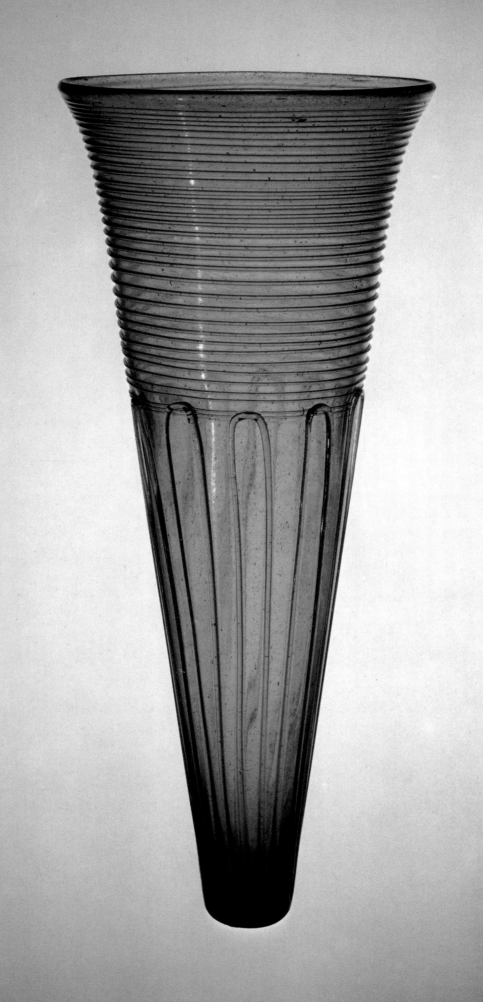

21

Frankish Cone Beaker

The withdrawal of Roman forces from Germany in the fifth century and the gradual decline of Roman culture thereafter brought new tastes in glass. These made themselves felt in the general region dominated by the Germanic tribes, who were generically called Franks. This included modern Belgium, northern France, and by extension Anglo-Saxon Britain. Not only does a new range of shapes impose itself, but simple types of decoration that could be carried out at the furnace replaced the more sophisticated decorative techniques of cutting, engraving, and enameling, usually executed in workshops away from the glasshouse. This tendency may be seen in the cone beaker illustrated on the opposite page, one of the best examples of the superb results that the glassmaker could produce by the simplest means. The absolutely regular, but not mechanical, horizontal threading below the rim and the precise, taut, looped threading below produce a tension between the two parts of the glass that exactly complements its form, swiftly rising from a narrow base, then comfortably static in its ampler upper parts and gently spreading rim.

The cone beaker developed from a shorter, broader, and more stable late Roman beaker, and it probably reflects the drinking habits of the Germanic tribes, whereby a glass when empty was taken from the guest's hand and refilled. It was not normally set down on a table, and almost all the Frankish drinking-glass types have either a vestigial foot (no. 22) or none at all. In the Anglo-Saxon poem of *Beowulf* (which dates from about 1000, but records a story perhaps three hundred years older), when there is feasting in the king's hall, "now and then before the high courtiers, Hrothgar's daughter bore the ale cup to the nobles from end to end." In the same way, in the eleventh century, Harold Hardrada, King of Norway, "like the old kings before him, used to drink from an animal's horn and himself bear the ale from the high seat about the fire to empty the cup of remembrance with those whom he would honor." Glass drinking horns, made in the semblance of animal's horns, were being produced at much the same period as the Corning cone beaker, and no doubt reflect similar drinking customs.

The Corning beaker was excavated at Acklam, in Yorkshire, and is a rare instance of a glass of this type found outside the southern counties of England.

Probably Rhenish,
5th–early 6th century.
Height: 23.5 cm

22

Frankish Claw Beaker

When the Franks came to exercise more and more influence in the territories to the west of the Rhine, they became increasingly important customers to the glassmakers who remained, and it is likely enough that gradually some of the Teutonic tribesmen were themselves absorbed into the industry. This style did not, however, suddenly lose its character, and the traditional soda-glass made from ash imported from the Mediterranean apparently continued to be produced for hundreds of years after the collapse of Roman power. The decorative resources at the disposal of the glassmakers were limited to what they could themselves produce at the furnace. Simple mold blowing was practiced, usually in corrugated molds, the resultant ribbing being sometimes "wrythen" to give a diagonal slant to the ribs. Much use was made of trailed threading, sometimes in the same color (as here and in no. 21), sometimes of opaque white glass, usually marvered into the surface of the vessel. All these methods had been perfectly familiar in Roman glassmaking; however, one technique, which was only foreshadowed in Roman glass, was developed in Frankish times and brought to a pitch of virtuosity peculiar to this period. This was the use of hollow "claws"—trunklike projections usually arranged in two offset rows—to decorate the body of a beaker.

The method of making these claws has been much discussed, and a variety of solutions has been proposed, the most acceptable of which appears to be that originally propounded by the late W. A. Thorpe. According to Thorpe, the beaker was shaped on the blowing iron, and any trailing was applied at this stage. The glass was then allowed to cool sufficiently to make it so set as to resist further blowing. A hot blob of glass was then applied by an assistant. This melted the wall of the vessel (including any threading) immediately below where it touched, which could therefore be blown outward into a hollow claw and then hooked downward and pressed to the wall or foot of the vessel, the marks of the tool being still visible at the bottom of the claw. When both rows (starting with the upper one) had been completed, the beaker was taken on a rod (called a pontil), the blowing iron was then "knocked off," and the rim finished. In some instances the claws were further embellished by the application of a notched vertical ribbon.

The Corning beaker is said to have come from Nordeifel in Germany.

Probably Rhenish,
6th century.
Height: 17.7 cm

Sasanian Cylindrical Goblet

This tall, cylindrical beaker is decorated with alternating green and same-colored threads, the former being crimped, apparently with an instrument resembling a roulette. These decorative elements are bounded above and below by a single horizontal thread. The cylindrical body rests, exceptionally, on a low, spreading foot. The glass is stated to have come from Amlash and shows by its creamy-buff weathering its affinity with a number of glasses alleged to have been found in the Gilan district, to the southwest of the Caspian Sea, where Amlash itself is situated. Predominant among these glasses is a series of straight-sided, wheel-faceted bowls that had a wide distribution in the Near and Middle East and were even traded as far afield as Russia on the one hand and Japan on the other. (These and other faceted glasses are discussed under nos. 24, 25.)

Along with the faceted bowls, however, a number of types of glass occur that are not wheel cut when cold but decorated at the furnace. Notable among these are a number of hemispherical bowls with decoration in the form of fins, or prunts, pinched out of the substance of the glass material by the glassmaker's tongs. One bowl of this kind has been found in a tomb at Hassain-mahaleh in the Dailaman area of the Gilan province. It has a row of triangular fins around the lower part of the bowl, and a row of horizontal prunts around the upper part of the body, while the bowl itself stands on a circle of ten toes nipped out of the base. A bowl of comparable shape, decorated with eight ribs in low relief and eight toes, was found in excavations in a third- to fourth-century cemetery at Tel Mahuz, some twenty-five miles from Kirkuk in northern Mesopotamia, and a further series of these bowls has been found in uncontrolled excavations in northwestern Iran, some standing on pinched toes, others on a base ring or solid disc foot. The bowl standing on toes and with pinched decoration is fairly common in Syrian, and indeed western, Roman glass of the third and fourth centuries, and examples of both bowls and flasks with this type of decoration occurred at Dura-Europos. Their presence there guarantees a date before the middle of the third century A.D., and shows that the type was in favor in this caravan city on the confines of Mesopotamia and Syria, balanced between the spheres of influence of Rome and Sasanian Persia.

It seems that in Mesopotamia, the most ancient center of glassmaking known, there was in the late Imperial Roman period an ambivalence of taste that accepted both the unmistakably Roman style of glassmaking in the Syro-Palestinian area, and a style that was specifically Iranian in its choice of forms and decoration. In northwestern Iran a similar duality of taste is apparent in the prevalence of the bowl with fins, and a disposition to accept foreign and exotic models may be discerned in Corning's tall goblet, which appears to be an adaptation of a form familiar elsewhere in the Near East (notably Egypt) in the fourth century, but also in Europe in that and the preceding century. The eastern examples are usually decorated with engraving, but also rarely with gilding and enameling, those from Europe with applied trailed and notched threads distinctly reminiscent of those decorating the Corning glass, although usually disposed in scrolling overall designs.

Northwestern Persia or northern Mesopotamia, probably 4th century. Height: 28.4 cm

24

Sasanian Cut Glass Vase

This vase belongs to a large class of glasses found in northwestern Iran which are decorated with wheel-cut facets. In the upper portion of the body of the vase, the facets are relatively shallow, circular, and spaced out; lower down, they are cut more deeply and are arranged so that they form an overall honeycomb mesh. Toward the base, the facets become larger until at the bottom seven circular cuts surround a central deep facet that is of greater diameter than any of the others. This feature recurs repeatedly in a large family of hemispherical, wheel-faceted bowls, the prototypes for which were found in quantity at Dura-Europos, fifty miles or so north of the Mesopotamian border with Syria. Dura was an important city on the trade route from the east which continued westward to Palmyra and Damascus.

At the other geographical extreme, bowls of this general kind have been found in Japan, where one example was excavated in the tomb of an emperor who died in 535, while a second is in the famous Shōsōin treasure house at Nara, the contents of which were dedicated in 756. To the north, a comparable bowl was found in the Urals in a context probably of the third or fourth century, while to the south, sixth-century examples were discovered at Kish, not far from Babylon; sixth- to seventh-century pieces were recovered from the Sasanian capital city of Ctesiphon, on the Tigris River below Baghdad. It is evident therefore that bowls of this kind had a wide distribution geographically and extended over a considerable period of time. It is reasonable to suppose that the vases, of which there are a small number known (in Leiden, Copenhagen, and Japan), were made during much the same period. It has been pointed out that the base of one of these vases, if cut off, would virtually constitute one of the hemispherical bowls.

There is some controversy over the method by which the pieces in this family were made. It has been suggested that they were molded, but this vase shape would be one virtually impossible to mold without blowing into a two-piece mold. It has also been suggested that they might have been cut from a solid block of glass, a procedure involving unwarranted difficulty in an age when glassblowing was a craft widely diffused throughout the civilized world and virtually certainly also practiced in Iranian territory (no. 23).

These pyriform vases follow closely in shape the ewers and vases made in semiprecious stones and in silver during the Sasanian period.

Northwestern Persia
or northern Mesopotamia,
6th–7th century
or earlier.
Height: 20.3 cm

27

Islamic Relief-cut Bottle

Allusion was made under the previous item (no. 26) to fragments of crystal glass found in Samarra, Iraq, capital of the Abbasid caliphate for some forty-five years in the ninth century. Some of these were decorated with running animals rendered in notched, raised outlines, which were produced by grinding back the surface of the glass. The bottle shown here illustrates other features of this style. Two running mouflon goats with curled horns confront each other on either side of a central motif consisting of S-shaped scrolls terminating below in a palmette. The eye of each animal is rendered as a relief dot in a shallow depression, reminiscent of the relief-cut umbilical bosses of Sasanian times (no. 25); the hip joint of the rear leg is marked with a notched scroll, and the flat surfaces of the front hoof and muzzle are hatched.

Whereas the Samarra beasts formed a frieze around the vessel, however, these goats confront each other on either side of what is probably a version of the Persian *homa*, or Tree of Life. The same rather static formula is to be found on the famous Egyptian rock crystal carvings of the Fatimid period (969–1171), where animals confront each other on opposite sides of a scrolling composition of palmettes and half-palmettes. Rock crystal bottles of the same shape as the Corning piece and with decoration purely of palmette motifs are also known; a crystal glass fragment from Egypt, now in the Victoria and Albert Museum in London, is decorated with the figure of a running animal combined with palmette motifs, all rendered in the same manner as the themes on the Corning bottle. These seeming ties with Egypt are probably more apparent than real.

In the Treasury of the Cathedral of St. Mark's in Venice is a bowl of opaque, turquoise-colored glass, presented by the shah of Persia to the Venetian Signoria in 1472, but evidently of much earlier date. This piece is decorated with a frieze of running animals engraved in relief in a manner very close to that of the glasses already discussed. It has an inscription in Kufic that has been read as "Khurasan." The province of Khurasan was famous for its turquoise mines, and it seems evident that turquoise glass (of which other examples have been found in Persia) was being passed off as the precious natural stone, much as the glasses discussed here might have been regarded as acceptable substitutes for the precious rock crystal. The bowl in St. Mark's provides good evidence that relief-cut glass was made in Iran during the Abbasid period (750–1258). The resemblance between the presumed Iranian glasses and those found in Iraq and Egypt is almost certainly to be put down to the unifying influence and the prestige of the caliphate, which at this time set the fashion for the Islamic world.

The glass of the Corning bottle shows much of the material quality referred to by the writers of the age, and its cutting is of the finest quality, even though it may lack some of the crispness and vigor of the Corning bowl (no. 28). The meticulous attention to detail, even in parts that are not normally visible, is to be remarked here in the internal bevel of the neck and the beautifully ground-out convex base within the foot ring.

Probably Iranian,
9th–10th century.
Height: 16.6 cm

Islamic Relief-cut Bowl

One of the revelations of recent years has been the emergence of a great number of Islamic glasses with wheel engraving of superb quality on a virtually flawless color-less crystal glass. Although provenances that depend on information transmitted through the art market are notoriously untrustworthy, the great majority of these pieces seems to come from northeastern Persia, and particularly the great city of Nishapur in Khurasan, where systematic archeological excavation produced glasses to match those derived from illicit digging in the same area. Previously found glasses of this general type were usually attributed to Ray or neighboring Sava, Ray having been the most important tenth-century city of the Jibal province. The tenth-century poet Abu Mansur Muhammed ben Ahmad al-Daqiqi, of Tus in Khurasan, compares a glass vessel to ice and water in point of clarity, thereby making it clear that crystal glass was a familiar phenomenon in contemporary Iran.

Where these glasses were made is an unsettled problem. Al-Harawi, a tenth-century author, wrote, "The diamond is a stone which resembles the crystal-glass of Baghdad," and a later Chinese text records that the products of Baghdad include "engraved glassware of finest quality." Several medieval texts refer to Iraqi glass by name, perhaps using the term as an appellation like "Venice glass," as was done in the sixteenth and seventeenth centuries in Europe. At Samarra, a number of fragments of the finest crystal cut glass have been excavated and may reasonably be dated to the ninth century, although Samarra is now known to have continued in occupation some time after the return of the caliph to Baghdad. It is known, more-over, that the Caliph al-Mu'tasim (833–842) had glassmakers brought from Basra to Samarra, presumably mainly for the supply of his own court. It may reasonably be assumed, therefore, that some of the finest Samarra glasses were made on the spot. Among these were sumptuous vessels engraved in relief with the figures of running animals. These were rendered by means of raised outlines, made by cutting back the surface of the glass on either side, then notching the resultant ridge.

The Corning bowl shown here is made of an almost colorless glass, although its exact quality is masked by heavy weathering. A slight tinge of color is here perhaps an indication of early date. In its present state it certainly does not invite comparison with rock crystal, but if its surface condition is imagined away, the quality of the engraving may be seen for what it is. The horizontal lines that bound the decorated field indicate the depth of glass that has been ground away to leave the figures stand-ing in relief. In the decorative frieze around the sides, four birds alternate with four ibex, which in some features, such as the hatching on the mane, are fairly close to the examples found at Samarra. On the base, two falcons flank a Tree of Life motif, formed of a central boss reminiscent of the boss cutting on earlier Sasanian glass, standing between a notched palmette above and a pair of scrolls below. Some of the characteristics of this style of relief engraving are discussed in entry no. 27, and here it is necessary only to draw attention to the vigor of the decorative scheme and the crispness and precision of the execution, qualities usually to be found in the early stages of a developing art.

The Corning bowl is said to have been found at Gurgan, a town near the south-eastern corner of the Caspian Sea. The modern town of Gurgan was known in early times as Astarabad, and was in Tabaristan, a neighboring province of Khurasan, not far from Nishapur itself.

Probably Iranian,
9th century.
Diameter: 14 cm

Hedwig Glass

The Legend of St. Hedwig (d. 1243), patron saint of Silesia, records that her husband, Duke Heinrich I, upon hearing from a court official that his wife as a part of her program of self-denial drank nothing but water, became concerned that this might be contributing to her ill-health. Determined to test the truth of the allegation for himself, he arrived unexpectedly at his wife's table and "took up the beaker which was set before her [filled] with water and drank from it: then he discovered in his mouth the taste of delicious wine which came from nothing but mere water. . . ." This miracle, with its reminiscence of the Feast at Cana, assured that, after the canonization of St. Hedwig in 1267, a number of glasses were associated with the saint and came to be treated as relics and to be mounted in metal as chalices.

Of these glasses those with the best claim to a connection with St. Hedwig are two beakers of the kind shown here, one in the Cathedral of Cracow, Poland, and a second in the Breslau Museum (the present Wroclaw, in Silesia, Poland). Both are roughly engraved with heraldic lions facing the spectator, in the manner of the Corning glass, but in addition the Cracow beaker bears the figure of an eagle with spread wings, while on the Wroclaw example the lions face a curious cuplike motif topped by a crescent with three stars. From these two examples, the whole family of such glasses, characterized by their shape, their usually smoky brown or green material, and their distinctive style of engraving, have acquired the name "Hedwig glasses." A number of those which have no connection with St. Hedwig nevertheless were mounted as reliquaries during the Middle Ages or the sixteenth century, an indication of the esteem in which they were held at the time. The decoration of this glass appears to be entirely wheel cut. The depth of the relief is distinctive, the whole ground of the glass being cut back to leave the ornamentation in relief above the surface. Internal details have sometimes been rendered in the same relief technique, but more often with hatching effected by light incisions in the intaglio technique.

Controversy surrounds the questions of the origin and dating of these glasses. Most of the fourteen surviving glasses have been preserved in church treasuries or aristocratic collections in Europe, from the confines of Germany in the west to Cracow in the east. More recently, however, a fragmentary example was excavated at Novogrudok, in Kievan Russia. None has been found in the Near East, and in consequence the group has been claimed both as Russian and as Byzantine. It seems, however, inescapable that wherever these glasses were made they represent the end of a long tradition of Near Eastern glass and hardstone engraving. Relief cutting (*Hochschnitt*) is the characteristic technique of a whole school of engraving in Persia (and perhaps also Mesopotamia) in the ninth and tenth centuries, and a favored theme was a frieze of running animals—deer, hares, lions—with hatched manes or necks, leaf-shaped feet, and tufted tails, the eye always rendered as a dot in relief and the joint of the thigh often emphasized by a scroll.

The famous rock crystals of Fatimid Egypt almost certainly represent a continuation of this tradition and probably overlapped with it. Much of this rock crystal engraving was probably done in Egypt itself, and there is growing evidence for the popularity of relief engraving on glass in Egypt in the ninth century. It is uncertain when rock crystal engraving declined in Egypt, but it was probably toward the end of the eleventh century. It seems eminently reasonable to suppose that when this luxury craft waned, the craftsmen should have turned their skills to the cheaper medium of glass. There are, in fact, Egyptian glasses wheel engraved on a brown material resembling that of the Hedwig beakers, and brown- and green-toned glasses are commonplace in Egyptian-Islamic finds. One of them is decorated with a running animal and a palmette relief-cut reminiscent of the pieces of the Hedwig family.

The Corning beaker originally came to light in the Sacristy of Halberstadt Cathedral, and for a time was used as a gluepot before passing into the collections of the Landesmuseum, Gotha, Germany.

Probably Egyptian,
late 11th–12th century.
Height: 8.6 cm

Drinking Horn of Lustred Glass

Egypt's most important single contribution to the art of glass in Islamic times was undoubtedly the discovery of lustre stains, a discovery that had far-reaching effects, particularly on the pottery industry of the Near East. Fragments displaying an astonishing range of colors and techniques have been recovered from Egyptian soil, but the majority of pieces are painted in a range of browns and yellows of precisely the same character as the yellow stain much used on European stained glass from about 1300 onward. This color was derived from sulphide of silver painted on the glass and then fired in a furnace in a reducing (smoky) atmosphere.

Egypt's claim to be the first center to produce lustred glass has been reinforced by a recent discovery at Fustat (the Islamic capital from 642 until 969, when it was gradually eclipsed by Cairo). A bowl excavated here bears an inscription relating to a certain 'Abd as-Samad, who was great-uncle to the legendary Harun al-Rashid, was governor of Egypt in 771–72, and died in 801. The bowl, therefore, can be certainly dated to the second half of the eighth century. In the last thirty years glasses with lustred decoration have also been uncovered in Iran, particularly in the great city of Nishapur, and although it is possible that they were imported from Egypt, they appear in fact to have a somewhat different character from that of the glasses excavated in Egypt. The picture has been even more complicated by the recent find of a bowl lustre-painted and inscribed, ". . . this cup was made in Damascus." Ties between Syria and Egypt, however, were very close at this time.

The Corning horn is painted with heart-shaped and torchlike motifs from which diverge sprays of blobby leaves, sometimes in a trefoil grouping with bracts(?) rendered as strokes across the stems. The character of this painting, which recurs on other Egyptian glasses, is also familiar from the lustre-painted pottery of the Fatimid period.

Drinking horns have a long history in glass, from Roman rhytons (drinking or pouring vessels) of the first century A.D. to the north European and Italian horns of as late as the sixth and seventh centuries A.D. However, there seem to be no immediate parallels for the Corning horn in the Islamic world.

Probably Eygptian,
9th–11th century.
Length: 23 cm

31

Bottle with Mold-blown Decoration

One of the most widespread techniques for the decoration of glass since the invention of glassblowing has been that of blowing the glass parison into a patterned mold. The mold was impressed with a formal pattern, such as ribbing or a mesh design, which after the glass was removed from the mold was expanded by blowing so that the design became softer, fainter, and more agreeable; or after removal the glass was twisted, which in the case of ribbing gave a spiral effect. The bubble of glass also could have been blown into a composite mold of two or more parts to take up a complicated design that only would have been distorted and spoiled by further working. Such designs include figures, inscriptions, or the representation of natural forms. The bottle illustrated here is decorated with a frieze formed by a running plant scroll above an inscription.

Traditionally, mold blowing has been associated with Syria, but it was certainly practiced in other lands of the Islamic Near East, too. A series of small mold-blown ewers is known that bear makers' marks, and some of these appear to include the formula "made . . . in Baghda[d]," while the only known clay molds for glass-blowing, of Islamic date, come from Iraq. A great majority of the mold-blown vessels coming onto the art market since World War II, however, have come from Iran, and it seems possible that a center of production of such wares was located in or near Gurgan, to the southeast of the Caspian Sea.

The Corning bottle is decorated, for good measure, with an applied band of zigzag threading, characteristic of medieval glasses coming from Iran.

Probably Iranian,
11th–12th century.
Height: 25.8 cm

79

32

Mamluk Enameled and Gilt Vase

One of the chief glories of Near Eastern glassmaking in the Middle Ages was the production of enameled and gilt glass in a profusion and a perfection of technique not equaled until Renaissance Europe witnessed the emergence of Venetian glass of comparable type (no. 34).

Some of the earlier glasses of this kind, decorated with rich, thick enamels and figures on a relatively large scale, were probably made in Aleppo, near the area where glassworkers from Armenaz (near Tyre) are said to have settled. The glasses that they made were supposedly brought into Aleppo to be decorated. The supremacy of Aleppo may have passed to Damascus when the Emir al-Nāsir Yūsuf II fled before Hulagu Khan to the latter city in 1250. Al-Nāsir was killed in 1260, but the glass industry continued to be prosperous until the city was destroyed by Tamerlane (Timur) in 1400, and the glassworkers were removed to Samarkand. The standing of Damascus as a glassmaking center in the fourteenth century before this calamity, however, was unquestioned. Symon Simeonis gave an account of his pilgrimage in the years 1325–26: "Concerning the wealth of this city, however, which shows forth particularly in gold and silver, cloth of gold and silks . . . in gold, silver, and bronze vessels incomparably fashioned with great art in the Saracenic manner, in glasses most pleasingly decorated, which are commonly made in Damascus . . . we forbear to write; for they cannot be captured on paper, nor set forth in words." That this glass was indeed decorated by enameling seems likely from the account of another European traveler, Ser Niccolo da Poggibonsi, who was in Syria in 1345–46 and who refers to "the street of the glass-painters." Later still (1384) another Italian visitor, named Frescobaldi, describes the division of the city into different quarters for different crafts and stresses the high degree of perfection in the arts ensured by the requirement that a son should follow his father's profession. In medieval European inventories the most commonly occurring epithet for a rare exotic glass is "de Damas."

The extremely rare vase illustrated here shows a division of the decoration into horizontal friezes, with motifs in roundels on a ground of formal ornament painted in red outlines filled in with gold and enlivened by touches of bright, thick enamel. The lowest and the uppermost zones are filled with rows of fish diagonally arranged, also painted in red outline. These fish, emblems of good luck and perhaps considered an assurance against poison, were a favored theme on Syrian enameled glasses. The most important frieze, around the body of the vase, shows decorative roundels enclosing arabesques and interrupting an emphatically painted inscription that consists of a repetition of the words "Al-'alim"("the Wise"). In the zone above this, four medallions enclose lotus heads, a clear sign of the Chinese influence on Near Eastern art in the period following the incursions of the Mongols from central Asia. The uppermost band has two roundels each enclosing a six-petaled rosette, probably the heraldic emblem of the owner. The elaborately looped handles are a reminder of the traditional skill of the Syrian glassblower in this sort of manipulative work.

Syrian, probably Damascus;
c. 1320–30.
Height: 30.2 cm

33

Enameled and Gilt Mosque Lamp from Cairo

One of the most important, and no doubt lucrative, branches of the Syrian glass industry was the supply of mosque lamps mainly to the mosques of Cairo. The sultans of the combined Egyptian-Syrian dominions and their chief officers competed with each other in the founding and embellishing of mosques and madrasehs (educational establishments) in the capital, and a high proportion of existing mosque lamps are known to have come from such pious foundations. The Italian traveler Frescobaldi, who visited Cairo in 1384–85, records that "Their mosques are all white inside, with great numbers of lamps burning."

The mosque lamp was not strictly a lamp but a decorative holder for a light, and some have a central tube into which a candle was most likely fixed. Most, however, probably housed a separate bowllike lamp in which a wick floated on oil. The lamps were normally suspended by three or six chains, depending on the number of "ear handles" provided. If the height of the building was considerable, the chains often ran together and were connected at a hollow ovoid bulb also made of enameled and gilt glass. Apart from their decorative appeal, these lamps also fulfilled a symbolic function, and are sometimes, as here, inscribed with a passage from the Koran: "God is the light of the Heavens and the Earth: His light is as a niche in which is a lamp, the lamp in a glass, the glass as it were a glittering star."

The Chinese-inspired lotus blossom, which on the Corning vase (no. 32) was confined within a medallion, here luxuriates, and with leaves and other flowers it occupies the main area of the body. A mosque lamp in the Victoria and Albert Museum on which this decoration runs riot all over both body and foot is known to come from the madraseh of the Sultan Hasan, built between 1356 and 1363. From the reign of the same sultan come a number of lamps bearing the heraldic cup emblem seen on the Corning lamp, probably referring to the Emir Saichu, the sultan's cupbearer, who built a cloister and a mausoleum in 1355.

The relatively perfunctory painting that is common on many of these lamps, and which became more pronounced as the century progressed, was probably partly due to the realization that detail was not easily visible from the ground when the lamps hung high.

Syrian, probably Damascus;
c. 1355.
Height: 30.5 cm

34

Cristallo Goblet with Enameled and Gilt Decoration

Relatively colorless clear glass had been made in Italy (not necessarily only in Venice) as early as the thirteenth century, but it seems to have experienced a revival in Venice about the middle of the fifteenth century. Called *cristallo* from its resemblance to the colorlessness of rock crystal, it was from this time onward often used in conjunction with colored glass (especially blue, but occasionally green or purple), and later by itself, in the making of vessels intended for decoration by gilding and enameling. Enameling, too, had been known in Venice at the end of the thirteenth century, but it appears to have fallen into disuse until revived at about the same time as the making of *cristallo*.

Decorating a glass by means of enameling was a lengthy matter. The gold was applied in leaf form as the last process of making the glass itself and was welded to the surface in the heat of the furnace. The glass was then annealed and sent to the decorator's studio, whether inside or outside the glasshouse, where it was painted with enamels. The enamels were often laid over the gold leaf, particularly in dotted borders, and the gold was usually incised with a point, as here, to contribute to the overall design. The glass was then carefully inserted into the coolest part of the annealing furnace and gradually heated until it could be picked up on the solid iron pontil rod. It was then submitted to the full force of the furnace until the enamels shone in the flame. The glass was then withdrawn, knocked off the pontil, and returned to the lehr (annealing furnace) for re-annealing.

The decoration of the earliest enameled glasses appears first to have been drawn from late medieval Gothic themes. With the waxing Renaissance, motifs derived from classical antiquity were increasingly favored, particularly the grotesques inspired by the then recently discovered wall paintings of the Roman Imperial period. The winged *putti* riding on garlands, vertical trophies of scrollwork, crossed shields, etc., issuing from classical vases and seen on the Corning goblet, are all derived from classical sources—perhaps by way of contemporary decorative engravings by north Italian artists such as Agostino Veneziano or Nicoletto Rosex da Modena. The names of some of the Venetian enamelers are known, but it has not so far been possible to make any certain attributions to them.

In shape this noble glass is close to one in the Dresden Museum, dated 1511 and made for Jörg von Kopidlnansky.

Venetian,
early 16th century.
Height: 23.6 cm

84

35

Lattimo Bowl with Enameled and Gilt Decoration

Chinese porcelain was known in Italy at least as early as the thirteenth century, when objects of identifiable Sung-dynasty types were in use in Lucera, in southern Italy. These had monochrome glazes of various tones, but in the fourteenth century, wares of this type were superseded by a white porcelain with usually blue underglaze painted decoration that dominated the ceramic production of the Ming dynasty (1368–1644). This porcelain gradually percolated through to the Near East and thence in isolated examples to Europe, where it made a profound effect by virtue of its whiteness, its hardness, its translucency, and the beauty of its blue painted decoration.

In the Middle Ages Venice was the main intermediary in east-west connections, and the Treasury of St. Mark's in Venice possesses a piece of Chinese porcelain of the Sung period. It was therefore natural that some of the earliest-recorded recipients of Chinese porcelain in the West should have been the Venetian Doges, beginning with Francesco Foscarini in 1442 and Pasquale Malipiero in 1461. It was equally natural that efforts should have been made in Venice to copy this fabulous material and its decoration, and not only did the makers of *maiolica* (tin-glazed pottery) turn to decorating their wares with blue designs *alla porcellana* ("in the porcelain manner"), but the glassmakers also entered the field. They had a material already in hand in the opaque white glass (*lattimo*, from *latte*, the Italian word for "milk") that had been made in Venice as early as 1359. This material, opacified with tin oxide, was white or creamy and slightly translucent, thus displaying two of the characteristics of porcelain, and it could be decorated with enamels and gold by the techniques described in the previous entry (no. 34). Frequently, the decoration of these rare pieces includes scrollwork and other motifs in blue that are clearly inspired by the imported porcelain. A document of 1504 records the purchase in Venice of "seven bowls of counterfeit porcelain," and it is reasonable to suppose that these may have been made in *lattimo*.

The Corning bowl, although possibly influenced by Chinese porcelain in its form, is decorated in wholly western style, with the head of a young man in front of whom flutters a ribbon bearing the device "EGO VOBIS SERVO SON," a garbled mixture of Latin and Italian that may be translated "I am your servant." The rendering of the head resembles closely that of a number of pictures by the Venetian artist Vittore Carpaccio (active from 1490 until his death in 1523/6). A second *lattimo* bowl with the same external scale decoration as the Corning bowl is in the Kunsthistorisches Museum in Vienna, and this bears in the center the head of a girl, with a ribbon inscribed "AMOR MASALIE" ("Love assails me"). The girl's head is even more obviously in Carpaccio's style, and it must be concluded that the painter of the bowls had had occasion to study this artist's work. The two bowls indeed may even form a pair of *coppe nuziali* (marriage cups), given as presents at the time of a wedding or engagement.

Venetian,
c. 1500.
Height: 5.9 cm.
Diameter (rim): 14.1 cm

36

Waldglas Beaker

At some date in the late Dark Ages the glassmakers of northern Europe turned away from the imported Mediterranean soda ash (no. 22) for their fluxing agent, no doubt because it was no longer available to them, and used the wood ashes that were the natural product of their own wood-burning furnaces. The resultant potash-lime glass, with more or less greenish or yellowish coloring from the iron impurities in the sands used, continued in use throughout the Middle Ages. Because the glasshouses that made it were situated in the woodlands that provided their fuel, the glass was called *Waldglas*, or forest glass. Probably in the fifteenth century the glassmakers first began to exert themselves to make the glass of better quality by more careful purifying of the ashes. The resultant beautiful glossy green glass, sometimes inclining to bluish tones, began to be cultivated for its own aesthetic value. That the glassmen of this period also were able to make a decolorized "white" glass is proved by their production of virtually colorless glass for windows, and it is in fact known that the green color was deliberately cultivated. Pastor Mathesius, who will be quoted in this volume more than once (no. 45), is our witness to this fact. In 1562 he writes of his own district of Joachimsthal in western Bohemia: "Since, however, glass is of its nature white and shining, especially if the sand and ashes are clean and have been diligently boiled and skimmed, people in these parts have commonly for wine made green glass in which a measure of fine shining wine looks fair and pleasing, and which gives the wine a gay color." He adds that this green tone was obtained by the use of copper oxide.

The beaker illustrated here is of a shape found in the late fifteenth and early sixteenth centuries, normally decorated with two or more rows of prunts drawn out into spinelike forms. A prototype of this kind of beaker, however, has been found in Bohemia in an archeological context of the late fourteenth or early fifteenth century, and a beaker decorated with milled threading very like that of the Corning beaker (but with the addition of blue threads) was used as a reliquary in the Church of St. Nicholas at Wismar as early as the year 1459.

German,
late 15th or
early 16th century.
Height: 10.3 cm

37

Covered Cristallo Cup

Venetian glassmaking is often associated with elaborate shapes and modes of decoration, but there was a moment in its history when understatement and elegance predominated. The covered cup illustrated here is made of a typical "colorless" glass with a slight brownish tinge, characteristic of Venetian *cristallo* glass of the sixteenth and seventeenth centuries. Its only ornament is the soberly worked cover finial that crowns the smooth sweep of its upper surface, which the lowest disc of the finial accentuates by cutting straight across it, just as the rim of the cover provides an accent to the uninterrupted line of the flaring beaker. The internal flange of the cover discreetly shadows both the diagonal line of the beaker wall and the horizontal of the cover itself.

The whole wall is scored and scribbled with the diamond-scratched graffiti of innumerable members of some German brotherhood or society, the earliest signature dating from 1574, others from as late as the eighteenth century. (The probably original wooden case bears the unverifiable date "1545" in ink.) A glass of this sort evidently lent itself well to the festivities of corporate bodies, for a beaker of virtually identical type is shown in a picture by Cornelis Anthonisz. of Amsterdam (c. 1499–c. 1556) representing a banquet of seventeen members of the Civic Guard. This painting, which is in the Rijksmuseum, Amsterdam, is dated 1533. Corning's beaker probably was used for festive occasions, indicated by the fact that its original spreading folded foot at some time had to be replaced in silver.

This type of beaker was evidently favored in the sixteenth-century Netherlands, for apart from the Anthonisz. painting a glass of this shape recurs constantly—sometimes with and sometimes without its cover—in the paintings of Joos van Cleve (c. 1485–1540). This was clearly a treasured studio prop which survived to be used again and again in his stereotyped renderings of *The Virgin and Child with St. Joseph.*

Venetian,
c.1530.
Height (with
cover): 29 cm

38

Wineglass

If a true classic is considered an object that is perfect in the harmonious balance of its constituent parts and in the complete aptness of its component forms to the material from which it is made, then some of the Venetian glasses of the middle years of the sixteenth century may perhaps lay a stronger claim to this status than any made since the Romans, or before the heyday of glassmaking in England at the beginning of the eighteenth century.

The glass illustrated here is made from three bubbles, or parisons, with two discs that separate bowl from stem and stem from foot. The stem is a hollow-blown column, swelling slightly toward the top and having an outer and an inner line of great elegance. The plain foot rises slightly in the center to give a concave curve taken up by the line of the lower part of the stem and by the superb sweep of the spreading bowl.

Glasses of pure forms like the present example are to be seen in the paintings of Paolo Veronese (c. 1528–88) dating from the third quarter of the sixteenth century, whereas the still-life paintings of the late sixteenth and early seventeenth centuries show glasses with much more complicated shapes, almost infallibly with various forms of decoration—mold-blown stems, broken ribbing around the base of the bowl, applied threads, gilding, and so forth. The phase of Venetian glassmaking represented by this glass appears to have been of relatively short duration, a moment of repose between the grandiose designs of the early sixteenth century and the progressively more fretful and sometimes positively fussy glasses of the Baroque. Such simple glasses show the glassmaker's direct response to the qualities of his prime material without recourse to accessories of any kind other than his basic kit of tools.

Venetian,
mid-16th century.
Height: 17.8 cm

39

English Goblet in the Façon de Venise

Until the middle of the sixteenth century the only clear and virtually colorless glass known in England had been imported from Venice. There are indications of glass-making by Venetian glassmen in the reigns of Henry VIII and Edward VI, but few details are known, and it seems unlikely that much, if any, Venetian-style glass was made there in this period. In 1567, however, a merchant from Antwerp named Jean Carré set up a furnace in London under license from the Corporation of London, and later in the same year he applied to Queen Elizabeth for a monopoly of making "crystal" glass. The application was turned down, but Carré probably continued work at his furnace until his death in 1572. Antwerp was at this time the leading center in northern Europe for the making of glass in the Venetian style, and from this city Carré obtained a number of his workers, notably one Giacomo Verzelini (1522–1606), a native of Murano who had lived for some years in Antwerp and married an Antwerp woman. On Carré's death Verzelini appears to have taken over the management of the glasshouse. In 1574 he applied to the queen for a patent in the manufacture of glass in the Venetian manner, and he was granted a monopoly of twenty-one years provided that he paid the queen's customs and made glass that would sell as cheaply as comparable foreign imports. In 1576 Verzelini took out papers of denization (that is, naturalization), which enabled him to become an owner of property and therefore to rebuild in his own name the furnace at the hall of the Crutched Friars in London that had probably been Carré's and which had been burned down in a disastrous fire the year before. Here he continued to produce glass until his retirement, probably in 1592.

A number of glasses in the *façon de Venise* have come to light in England which by virtue of their English inscriptions or other English connections may reasonably be attributed to Verzelini's glasshouse. This series consists of some nine intact glasses and a number of fragments. All but one are decorated by means of the diamond point, the exception being the latest of all, dated 1590, which is decorated in gilding with the arms of the Vintners' Company of London. The others range in date from 1577 to 1586, the former being a goblet in the Corning Museum engraved with the initials "RB" and "IB," presumably those of a husband and wife.

The goblet of 1583 illustrated here has the "round-funnel" bowl common to a number of the group, but is exceptional in having a hollow lion-mask stem, blown in a two-piece mold and showing two lion's heads in full face separated from one another by shields. Such lion-mask stems are commonplace in Venetian glassmaking of the sixteenth century, but this glass is the only example within the Verzelini group. The bowl of the goblet has been engraved with a series of motifs characteristic of these glasses: first, a border of arrowheads with double scrolls at their bases; then an in-scription "IN.GOD.IS.AL.MI.TRVST"; third, a zone in which upright panels enclosing leafy scrollwork alternate with three square panels, one enclosing initials "KY" joined by love knots, the second an elaborate merchant's mark, and the third the date 1583.

"In God is all my Trust," which occurs on this glass and another (dated 1586) in the series, may be the motto of the Pewterers Company, and one man who had a connection with the Pewterers at this time is recorded as a "graver in puter and glasse, borne under the obedyence of the French King." This man, named Anthony de Lysle, is recorded in April 1583, as a denizen (i.e., naturalized citizen) within the Liberty of St. Martin the Grand, in London. There seems little doubt that de Lysle engraved the Corning goblet and the other glasses in the Verzelini group.

English, London;
dated 1583.
Height: 20.9 cm

40

Covered Goblet with White-striped Decoration

Enameled and gilt decoration of glass began to go out of fashion probably toward the end of the first quarter of the sixteenth century. Its place was taken by a decorative technique which was intrinsic to the glass itself and entirely carried out in the glasshouse. Threads of opaque white (*lattimo*) glass had for centuries been applied in horizontal circuits to the surface of glasses by way of embellishment, but now they were embedded in the glass in a vertical arrangement. *Lattimo* canes or collapsed tubes (to give broad, flat stripes) were arranged vertically inside a cylindrical mold and picked up on a gather of clear, colorless glass. They were then marvered into the surface of the glass and worked with the rest of the parison, being first pinched together at the bottom so that when the surplus was cut off they appeared to radiate from a single point. Plain canes or tubes could be substituted by twisted cables, formed by picking up canes (usually four) in the way described, marvering and twisting them, and finally coating them with a layer of colorless *cristallo*. A cable normally alternated with a plain stripe, as here. The goblet is made in three sections—bowl, knop, and foot—with two plain discs, or "mereses," interposed. The finial of the cover is also made of plain glass.

It is difficult to say when this technique was first introduced. In 1527 two brothers, Filippo and Bernardo Serena, applied to the Venetian authorities for a patent for a new method of work involving "twists of cane" (*retortoli a fil*). This probably referred to the use of *lattimo* cables, usually described as work *a retortoli* or *a retorti*. It may be taken as axiomatic that when a patent was applied for, the basic idea had been practiced for some time previously. There is, in fact, one important glass with a knop decorated in this way that has a good claim to be of the late fifteenth century.

The glass illustrated here, with its extraordinary shape reminiscent of puffed and slashed hose, has a number of parallels, some with covers, some without. The shape is represented in a pattern book of the glasshouse at Beauwelz, in the southern Netherlands (present-day Belgium), dating probably from about 1550–55, and a similar glass is represented in a Netherlands still-life painting of about 1580. A slightly different glass, but with a bowl of the same complex profile, is seen in a still life by the Antwerp painter Osias Beert (about 1580–1624), and it must date from the early years of the seventeenth century. On the other hand, the same shape, usually in colored glass, is found embellished with enameling which seems to indicate for the glasses concerned an origin in Bohemia and a date in the last two decades of the sixteenth, or the first of the seventeenth, century. The general type was probably made in a number of centers working in the Venetian manner (*façon de Venise*) in central and northern Europe, but it seems certain that it was also made in Venice itself for customers in those areas.

Venetian or façon de Venise,
*late 16th or
early 17th century.*
Height (with cover): 34.9 cm

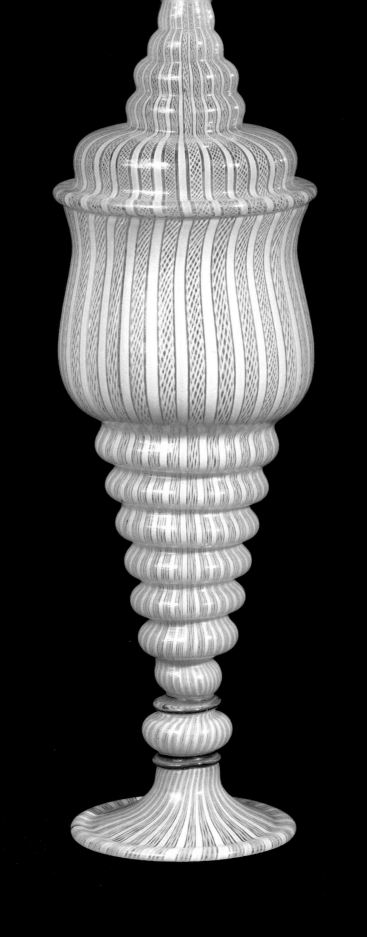

41

Drinking Glass with White-striped Decoration

The shallow bowl of this *tazza* is decorated with white stripes arranged in such a way that three plain bands alternate with a single cable; the same formula is observed in the hollow-blown baluster stem and in the foot. The three parts of the glass are separated by elements in plain glass, that between stem and foot covering the uneven end of the hollow baluster.

Glasses such as these, requiring a steady hand in the drinker, are often seen in Italian pictures of the sixteenth or early seventeenth century, and an example very similar to the glass illustrated here appears in the late sixteenth-century Netherlands still life referred to in the previous entry (no. 40). The best-known parallel is in the painting of *Bacchus* by Caravaggio, in the Uffizi Gallery, Florence, although the glass represented there is decorated with swirled mold-blown ribbing in place of the white stripes. This picture is thought to have been painted about 1595. It well suggests the difficulty of holding a glass of this shape when filled with wine.

An English traveler of the third quarter of the seventeenth century wrote: "Another day we went to *Murano* again to see the glasshouses which furnish almost all *Europe* with drinking glasses. They utter here forth two hundred thousand crowns worth a year of this britle wares; and they seem to have taken measure of every nations belly and humour, to fit them with drinking glasses accordingly. For the High Dutch, they have high glasses, called *Flutes*, a full yard long. . . . For the Italians that love to drink leisurely, they have glasses that are almost as large and flat as silver plates, and almost as uneasie to drink out of. . . ."

Venetian or façon de Venise,
late 16th or
early 17th century.
Height: 13.6 cm

42

Kuttrolf of Colorless Glass with Opaque White Thread Decoration

The container shown in this illustration combines a great number of the tricks available to the glassblower. The original parison has been thickened by a "second gather," the upper edge of which can be seen at the base of the neck. This was then decorated with vertical canes, made of twisted *lattimo* and colorless glass threads, left in relief on the surface. The neck, the upper part of the original parison, was then made by reheating all but the body and then sucking the air out of the flask creating three tubes grouped around a central tube, the vacuum causing the collapse of the softened part of the neck. The foot would then be made of a second parison, decorated with cables of the same design as those on the body but marvered flush with the surface. This parison would then be sheared off and turned under to form the foot rim. The glass would then be transferred to the pontil rod and the opening shaped and trimmed with a turn of opaque white glass.

This complex shape, usually called a *Kuttrolf*, has its origins in Roman times, when flasks with wide mouths were made much in the way described, usually with four tubes grouped around the constricted waist. From Roman times dates the origin of its name, the Latin *gutturnium* being essentially a vessel that allowed liquid to be dispensed a drop (*gutta*) at a time. In Germany a second word, *Angster*, ultimately derived from the Latin *angustum* (narrow), had a similar significance, and it is in practice impossible to know exactly what distinguished these two words in the German parlance of the Middle Ages and later. The *Kuttrolf* form shown here was used for drinking by pouring into the mouth in the manner of a Spanish *porró*. There was a second shape that used the inhalation technique to produce tubes around the body of the vessel or the base of the neck, and this was a bottle with narrow orifice for the storage and dispensing of liquids. Yet a third form had a narrow neck often curved, without tubes, and a wide flaring mouth; if the neck was curved, the mouth was usually lipped, as in the *Kuttrolf* illustrated, for pouring the liquid directly into the mouth. A Venetian long-necked flask, called from the thirteenth century onward *inghistera* (which derives its name from exactly the same root as the *Angster*), shows that to pour liquid drop by drop a flask did not need to have a many-tubed neck. This has merely a tall, narrow neck rising from an onion-shaped body usually on a foot. The multitubed vessel, however, was certainly made in Venice, too, and probably elsewhere in Italy, perhaps under the name *zuccarin*, in use from the end of the sixteenth century onward. The Venetian examples display a rich fantasy in the range of forms and variety of decoration.

Whether the Corning *Kuttrolf* was made in Venice for the German market or in Germany in some glasshouse working in the Venetian manner is impossible to know positively today. For the former attribution speak the applied foot and the general lightness and delicacy of touch; for the latter, the double gather of the body and the traditional shape.

Probably Venetian,
17th century.
Height: 25.1 cm.
Bequest of Jerome Strauss

43

Enameled Tazza

If any glassmaking center in the Mediterranean world could rival Venice in the fifteenth century, it was Barcelona. Glassmaking there was of great antiquity, and by 1455 the glassworkers were of sufficient significance to form a guild and to elect one member to the city council. In 1492 Jeronimo Paulo, writing to Paolo Pamphili in Rome, said that Barcelona glass, much esteemed at the court of Rome, rivaled that of Venice. A hundred years later a Catalán priest, Pere Gil, wrote in his manuscript *Natural History of Catalonia*: "The glass that today is made in Venice is considered excellent, but . . . in many ways, that made in Barcelona and other parts of Cataluña is better. . . ." Some allowance may be made for local patriotism, but in fact much of the glass that with some confidence can be attributed to Barcelona is of high quality and has an originality that acquits it of any mere imitation of Venetian styles. One facet of this originality is seen in its enameled glasses, which bear virtually no resemblance in either forms or styles of decoration to the contemporary glasses made in Venice.

Although the shape of the dish shown here reveals none of the eccentric features that distinguish some other Spanish glass shapes, the decoration is distinctive. Dominated in color by a fresh leaf green and by white, the painting depicts stylized hounds coursing through a landscape formed of conventionalized trees with blunt rounded or lanceolate leaves in the branches of which perch white birds. From the center medallion radiate jagged leaves between which are groups of two stamens on either side of a wavy line. Around the rim runs a continuous scroll border simulating leaves with fruit. This curiously naive style bears no resemblance whatever to the sophisticated Renaissance designs of Venetian enameled glass, but it reflects the hybrid *mudejar* style of Renaissance Spain with its admixture of Islamic and Gothic features. Technically, however, the Venetian and Catalán traditions seem to have been the same. Pere Gil is our witness that "Crystal glasses, when completely finished, are painted with green, gold, and other colors and returned to the furnace . . . for annealing; and that coloring remains fixed so fast that it can rarely, if ever, be separated."

In Venice, enameling and gilding seem to have gone out of fashion, except possibly on glasses for the northern market, in the second quarter of the sixteenth century. In Barcelona they continued in popularity until the middle of the following century, although there is a notable falling-off in quality toward the end.

Spanish, Barcelona;
c. 1560–1600.
Diameter: 22.6 cm

44

Lattimo-threaded Wineglass

Although the glassmakers of Spain are perhaps most renowned for the production of fantastic shapes, they could also produce glasses of a fastidious elegance and purity of form that rival the Venetian glasses of the mid-sixteenth century (no. 38). The wineglass illustrated here is decorated with applied opaque white threads in the Venetian manner (nos. 40 and 41), and there is record of a Spanish glassblower named Juan Rodriguez who practiced his craft in the years before 1537 in both Venice and Barcelona before returning to Seville to continue his life's work. Rodriguez was a native of Cadalso, in Castille, a great glassmaking center, as its full name of Cadalso de los Vidrios (Cadalso of the Glasses) clearly indicates. During his apprenticeship Rodriguez learned how to make *lo rayado a la manera de Venecia* (striped glass in the Venetian style), and although it is not made clear whether he learned this trick of the trade in Venice or in Barcelona, it may well be that he acquired it directly from the Muranese craftsmen, as the phrase would suggest. In fact, Spanish glasses with this type of decoration are not always executed in the Venetian technique, by which white threads picked up from a mold were pinched together into a single point and the surplus glass beyond this point cut off and discarded, so that all the threads radiated from a single center. In some Spanish-made glasses the opaque white glass is visibly looped below the base of the vessel, suggesting that the canes were trailed on the parison and not picked up from a mold in the normal Venetian manner.

It is known that glasses of this kind were in use in Catalonia during this period from an inventory taken at Vich (not far to the north of Barcelona) in 1581, which records a drinking glass with white lines (*bavedora de vidre ab ses vies blancas*); another lists the household goods of a Mallorcan doctor in 1616 and includes a drinking glass with white stripes (*bavedora ab rretxas blancas*).

Stripes of opaque white glass were used to decorate the glasses of Cadalso, as the career of Juan Rodriguez would imply, but the relatively colorless glass and the pure form of the Corning goblet strongly suggest an attribution to Barcelona. This level of quality no doubt explains why King Philip II of Spain was content to possess, alongside 320 Venetian glasses listed in the 1564 inventory of the Pardo Palace, no fewer than 263 glasses of Barcelona manufacture.

Spanish, probably Barcelona;
mid- or late 16th century.
Height: 17.8 cm

45

Beaker with Checkered Spiral-trail Decoration, White Enameling, and Gilding

Probably Bohemian, late 16th or early 17th century. Height: 16.5 cm

The beaker illustrated here has been decorated by a singular technique developed in the sixteenth century. A thick ribbon of glass was trailed spirally around the gather from bottom to top, the beginning of the trail usually being observable under the base of the resultant vessel, close to the pontil mark. The parison was then blown into a vertically ribbed mold that cut across the trail, breaking it up into a series of cushionlike facets resembling table-cut gems. After shaping, the vessel was normally given a foot rim consisting of a second thick trail laid around the basal angle, flattened, and often notched with a tool to give a milled effect.

In the case of the Corning beaker, the spiral decoration has been emphasized by a spot of white enamel painted between each pair of facets in their vertical rows, and a series of dotted vertical white lines breaking the horizontal rows. A number of other beakers with this combination of decorative tricks are known, being exclusively of the tall cylindrical form usually called in German *Stange* (or pole). When decorated by the spiral-trail technique, however, this shape has traditionally been called a *Spechter*, as a result of a passage from the famous "Sermon on Glass-making" contained in the book entitled *Sarepta, oder Bergpostill* by Johann Mathesius, published in 1562. Mathesius was not only the friend and biographer of Luther, but pastor of the Joachimsthal, a glassmaking district in western Bohemia (modern Czechoslovakia), and he shows a great familiarity with the glass industry of his time. In one passage he refers to ". . . the very smooth, pure, high and narrow green Spechters [that] are made in the Spessart [a district of Hesse], on which there are neither rings nor stones [that is, applied trails or prunts]. . . ." The interpretation of this difficult passage has always been open to doubt, but since Mathesius refers to the *Spechter* as being of green glass, it seems somewhat unlikely, apart from any other considerations, that he referred to the present class of glasses, which are exclusively a dark version of the Venetian *cristallo*.

Since white enameling, particularly in the form of dots, is frequently, if not exclusively, found on glasses that for a variety of reasons are attributed to Bohemia, it seems likely that the Corning beaker was made in that general area. The same beaker shape is found in colored glasses with polychrome enameling which can with reasonable certainty be ascribed to Bohemia and which often bear dates in the 1590s and the first decade of the seventeenth century.

46

Imperial Eagle Beaker

One of the most common themes used in the decoration of German enameled glasses was that of the *Reichsadler* or Imperial Eagle, usually painted on the large cylindrical beakers referred to as *Humpen*. This decoration symbolized the unity of the Holy Roman Empire, a unity that was more imaginary than real at the time when most of these beakers were made. The double-headed eagle itself was a symbol of the empire, and on its wings were displayed coats-of-arms representing the different orders of society. Along the tops of the wings run the arms of the electors, the three ecclesiastical electors (with the Holy See) on one side balancing the four temporal electors on the other; below them groups of shields are arranged vertically in fours, each group standing for a so-called *Quaternion*, or constituent element in the social order, starting with dukes and margraves and continuing down to villages and burgs. This classification, which never corresponded to political reality, was formulated in the fifteenth century, and its first pictorial representation dates to the end of that century. A version very like that found on the earlier *Humpen* is to be found in a print by Hans Burgkmair dated 1510. The crucifix shown on the earlier glasses, as here, is replaced later by an orb; the cross with serpent on the reverse of this glass is also an early feature. This *Humpen* is inscribed "Das Heilig Römisch Reich mit sampt seinen Glidern" ("The Holy Roman Empire with all its parts").

These huge glasses were in fact intended for drinking. A writer of 1616 gives the advice, "One should summon to oneself merry fellows and good friends, wipe the dust off the Romische Reich [i.e., the *Reichsadlerhumpen*] . . . and thus inspire and set on foot a jolly toping and tippling-party. . . ." A French visitor to Germany in 1688 provides this impartial commentary on German drinking habits, "You know the *Germans* are strange Drinkers; there are no People in the World more obliging, civil, and officious; but they have terrible Customs as to the Point of Drinking. . . . Every Draught must be a Health, and as soon as you have emptied your Glass, you must present it full to him whose Health you drank. You must never refuse the Glass, which is presented, but drink it off to the last Drop. Do but reflect a little on these Customs, and see how it is impossible to leave off drinking. . . . You must further know, that the Glasses are as much respected in this Country as the Wine is beloved. They place them all *en Parade* . . . and the glasses are ranged all about upon the Cornish [cornice] of the Wainscot, like Pipes of Organs. They begin with the little, and end with the great Ones; and these great Ones are always used, and must be emptied at a Draught, when there is any Health of Importance. . . ." Into this category the *Reichsadlerhumpen* undoubtedly fell.

Bohemian, dated 1574. Height: 26.4 cm

47

Enameled Hunt Goblet

Although enameling apparently began to go out of fashion in Venice itself during the second quarter of the sixteenth century, enameled glasses continued to be made there to cater to the demand in the countries of northern Europe. It was not very long, however, before the glassmakers in those areas began to practice the art themselves—probably in the Venetian-style glasshouses that had commenced work in the Austrian-Bohemian area—as early as 1486 in the case of Vienna, 1534 at Hall in the Tyrol, 1577 and later in various parts of Bohemia and Germany. Our earliest specific reference to glass enameling being practiced in this general area comes from Johann Mathesius (no. 45). In his book of sermons, *Sarepta, oder Bergpostill,* is a section devoted to glassmaking, a subject which would have been entirely familiar to his congregation and which he therefore used as a source of metaphor in his sermon.

There is in consequence every probability that what Mathesius says corresponds to the reality of work in the contemporary glasshouses of his part of the country: "Thereafter imagination has invented one new thing after another: some have caused all sorts of pictures and inscriptions to be fired in colors on the colorless glass in the annealing furnace, as the portraits and coats-of-arms of important gentlemen had been painted on window-panes. . . ." This passage not only shows that he regarded enameling on vessels as a transference from the craft of stained glass, but that the work was fired in the glassmaker's furnace, as was the practice in Venice itself (no. 34). Mathesius's words also suggest that the use of enamels on vessel glass was of relatively recent introduction. There are in fact a few enameled glasses of shapes popular in the German area and with German coats-of-arms that bear dates in the 1550s and 1560s, but examples become far more frequent from the 1570s onward.

The Corning goblet illustrated here belongs to a type of mainly blue, but occasionally colorless, glasses that bear dates in the 1590s and the first decade of the seventeenth century. The commonest shapes are globular jugs with cylindrical necks reminiscent in shape of contemporary German salt-glazed stonewares, tankards tapering from a broad base to a narrow mouth, beakers spreading from base to rim (with a milled foot-rim), stemmed goblets decorated with dangling rings, and the present form of goblet. This has a marked affinity in shape with a fairly common class of glasses decorated with opaque white threading (no. 40). The hunting subject that encircles the upper half of the glass belongs to one of the most popular categories of decoration in German glass. Such scenes were usually compiled by the painter from elements in the engravings of such artists as Virgil Solis, Jost Amman, and others.

Bohemian,
dated 1597.
Height: 27.2 cm.
Gift of Edwin J. Beinecke

48

Green Glass Roemer

For more than a hundred years controversy has raged over the origin and exact meaning of the word *Roemer*, which today is usually taken to mean a drinking glass, normally green, with a hollow cylindrical stem standing on a coiled foot, and with a more or less ovoid bowl rising from the top of the stem, from which it is normally marked off by a horizontal applied thread. The stem is usually decorated with prunts, either drawn out into thornlike projections (as here), or stamped with a raspberry or similar motif. However, this is probably a relatively recent concept, dating from the seventeenth or at earliest the middle of the previous century.

Documents dating from the 1450s, 1460s, and 1470s in Cologne mention *roemsche glaser*, or "Roman glasses"; and from 1512 onward until the middle of the sixteenth century, inventories in the same city list *roemer* or *roemergin* (little *Roemers*). This body of written material, dating from before 1550, stands in marked contrast to an apparently total dearth of references in other parts of Germany until the second quarter of the seventeenth century is reached. The exact meaning of the word *Roemer* in the early Cologne documents, however, is difficult to establish. It may be inferred from the contexts in which the word occurs that it was not a Venetian-type *cristallo* glass; that it came in different shapes and sizes; and that it was at least occasionally decorated with prunts. The term may well have been applied to different types of *Nuppenbecher* (prunted beakers) in green glass, which are known to have been in use in the fifteenth century (no. 36). The "Roman glasses" of that century are presumably to be equated with the *Roemer* of the sixteenth-century inventories, and the appearance of these terms specifically in Cologne is significant, for even in the fifteenth century the citizens of Cologne were proud of the Roman origins of their city—a city where the chances of finding actual Roman glasses were stronger than almost anywhere else. Since glasses with applied prunts and threads might well have been among any finds made in the soil of the city, the transference of the epithet "Roman" to prunted glasses of high quality would be perfectly natural.

Whatever the interpretation of its name, the *Roemer* became widespread in Germany during the late sixteenth and early seventeenth centuries. Enormous numbers of them were exported up the Rhine from the glasshouses of Hesse, Lorraine, etc. (no. 49), to be bought in Cologne by Dutch middlemen coming down from Amsterdam. In 1685 one of the middlemen, Tynnes Jacobs of Amsterdam, ordered no fewer than thirty thousand *Roemers* of two different kinds, in a total consignment of sixty thousand glasses, from the Laubach glasshouse in Hesse. This large-scale import is no doubt reflected in the frequent appearance of the *Roemer* in the still-life paintings of mid-seventeenth-century Dutch artists, who show it being used for the drinking of white (Rhenish) wine. A glass very like that illustrated here is represented in a still life dated 1634 by the Haarlem painter Willem Claesz. Heda (c. 1593–c. 1680); and an actual surviving glass almost identical to it is dated 1626 (Leiden Museum).

German,
probably first quarter
of 17th century.
Height: 27.8 cm

112

49

Roemer with Sepia (Schwarzlot) Enameling

In the second half of the seventeenth century a new type of glass decoration came to the fore in Germany. Although it was a new development as a means of ornamenting vessel glass, it was in fact no more than a transference to vessels of a technique that had been used by the painters of stained glass from the Middle Ages onward. Its greatest exponent, Johann Schaper, was a stained-glass artist before he turned his attention to decorating drinking glasses, and he went on to work in both fields. In the same way, a lesser-known artist, W. Spengler, who painted and signed a glass in Constance in 1683, is otherwise known only as a stained-glass artist.

Schaper came from northern Germany, and in this area, as in Holland, stained glass in the seventeenth century had become an art of painting on panels of colorless glass, much as a painter in oils painted on canvas. The range of transparent pigments was limited, but in any case painting in monochrome black (the age-old resource of the stained-glass artist in rendering outlines) appealed to the Puritan taste of the age in that part of Europe. Although Schaper did decorate a limited number of glasses in translucent enamel colors, by far his greatest achievement was his delicate rendering of landscape and figural themes in subtle gradations of his black enamel, the details picked out in the enamel with a fine point—the "stickwork" of the stained-glass artist. By 1655 Schaper had settled in Nuremberg. In 1658 he was admitted a Master in the Glaziers' Guild in Nuremberg, and he died there in 1670. A number of other artists in Nuremberg followed the fashion Schaper had set, but none could rival the suavity of his painting (often following prototypes in prints) or the delicacy of his linear point work.

Nuremberg, although the most important, was not the only center for this kind of painting. Mention has already been made of W. Spengler working in Constance, and a certain Johann Anton Carli (d. 1682) of Andernach painted and signed a series of goblets. Probably before the end of the seventeenth century the technique had spread to the Bohemian-Silesian area (no. 70).

Most of the German sepia-painted glasses referred to above were made of colorless "crystal" glass, and occasionally an opaque white or opalescent glass was decorated in *Schwarzlot*, but even this was exceptional. The small green *Roemer* shown opposite is therefore of considerable rarity. A second glass of the same kind in the Victoria and Albert Museum in London also has a marine subject—*putti* riding in cockleshell boats drawn by horses or propelled by a triangular sail. Marine subjects on the known German glasses are unusual, and it seems most likely that these green glasses were painted in Holland, a country where the sea was of paramount importance and where the technique of sepia painting was as familiar to the stained-glass artists as it was in Germany. We also know, from Dutch still-life paintings and from documentary evidence, that green *Waldglas Roemers* were greatly prized by the Dutch, who bought them in great quantities at Cologne. The glasses were brought to Cologne by barge from Frankfurt and other points on the river Main from the Hesse glasshouses at Laubach, Breitenborn, Paderborn, and probably many others, and from other glassmaking areas such as the Spessart, Swabia, and Lorraine (no. 48).

German (glass)
and Dutch (enameling),
late 17th century.
Height: 12.5 cm

50

Enameled Humpen

A great many enameled German glasses have political themes, notably those celebrating the unity of the Holy Roman Empire—the *Reichsadlerhumpen* (no. 46) and the two varieties of *Kurfürstenhumpen* (Elector *Humpen*) with their representations of the emperor amid his electors, in one case seated, in the other mounted on horseback. The *Humpen* shown here has a more specific theme—the Treaty of Westphalia, which in 1648 brought an end to the Thirty Years' War. The decoration shows God the Father leaning down out of Heaven to give a benediction on the three rulers depicted standing below on a cloverleaf—the emperor in the center, with the king of France (Louis XIV) on his right and the queen of Sweden (Christina) on his left. This curious composition is based on an engraving published by Matthäus Rembold in Ulm shortly after the conclusion of the peace. The passionate intensity of the relief felt after the long-drawn-out agony of probably the cruelest and most devastating war in European history to that date sounds through the wording of the long inscription on the reverse, beginning, "Thy Peace, Thy Peace, Thy divine Peace, take from us never again; let the same be handed down to our children and let it pass in inheritance to our posterity. . . ."

All the glasses commemorating this event seem to have been made and enameled in Franconia, where a number of glasshouses existed in the Fichtelgebirge range, just to the west of the Bohemian border; centers of enameling were certainly situated in the towns of Kreussen to the west and Bischofsgrün to the east. At Kreussen there was a manufacture of brown salt-glazed stoneware that was decorated in a bright palette of enamels dominated by the extensive use of white. This coloring is also characteristic of the glasses enameled in the region; on the glass illustrated may be noted particularly the use of white dots and strokes for the decorative borders and filling motifs. It is, however, impossible to be sure where a particular glass was made or enameled. These two processes were not necessarily carried out in the same place. However, it is known that at Bischofsgrün glasses were both made and enameled in the same glasshouse. Other examples of this design are known with dates as early as 1649 and as late as 1652.

German, Franconia,
dated 1650.
Height: 26.4 cm.
Gift of Edwin J. Beinecke

51

Butts Glass with White-striped and Enameled Decoration

Enameled glass was made in most parts of Germany and Bohemia, and it is very often difficult to decide in which area a particular glass was made. Some glasses, however, are distinguished by the subject matter of their decoration, and prominent among these are the so-called *Hofkellereigläser*, the glasses made for the butteries of castles belonging to various members of the Saxon princely house. Since these glasses, apart from their characteristic subject matter, are also painted in distinctively fresh enamels disposed in a light and open style, there is good reason to suppose that most were made in Saxony, even if an occasional example may come from the neighboring regions of Bohemia, Thuringia, and Franconia. Indeed, it is known that a glass dealer named Peter Hille, who came from Kreibitz in Bohemia, supplied glasses to the court in Dresden in 1599 and 1610, including on the first occasion "white-striped wine-glasses," which may very well have been of the general character of that illustrated here. The continuity in this type of glass is demonstrated by a glass in the Victoria and Albert Museum which is similar to the Corning piece except that the arms are those of Johann Georg I of Saxony and the date is 1623. The same type of glass seems to have been in use for a full fifty years after this, at a time when *lattimo*-striped glasses had virtually disappeared elsewhere in Europe.

The Corning glass bears on the front the full heraldic achievement of the Elector Johann Georg II of Saxony (ruled 1656–1680), with the initials "I.G.D.A.H.Z.S.I. C.V.B.C." for "Johann Georg der Andere Herzog zu Sachsen, Jülich, Cleve und Berg Churfürst" ("Johann Georg II Duke of Saxony, Jülich, Cleve and Berg, Elector"). Below the arms is the date "1662." On the reverse of the beaker is a representation of a target with a crossbow bolt in the bull's-eye, and the inscription "Haupt Schüsen Zu Dreszden" ("Main Butts, Dresden"). A set of glasses of exactly the same type are inscribed "Bey Einweiyung dess Neuerbauten Schiesshauses Anno 1678" ("For the Inauguration of the new-built shooting-range 1678"). A description of this actual occasion, which included a crossbow contest, survives: one of the members of the procession carried a "glass with a cover, painted in stripes, filled with Alicante wine, on one side of the glass the full Electoral coat-of-arms, with the Electoral bonnet above and the ribbon of the Order round it; on the other, a white paper [target] with a bolt on the mark, and above the words: 'For the Inauguration of the new-built shooting-range.'"

52

Purple Dish Engraved with the Diamond Point

Diamonds seem to have come into general European consciousness in the course of the fifteenth century, and a manner of faceting them by means of the lapidary's wheel appears to have been perfected in the Low Countries by 1476. At this time India was the only available source of the gems, and since most of the oriental trade of Europe then went through Venice, the properties of the diamond were probably familiar there at an early date. In 1549 Vincenzo di Angelo dal Gallo, of Murano, applied to the Venetian authorities for a patent covering his technique of engraving glass with the diamond point, which he alleged he had been practicing for fourteen or fifteen years. His application was granted, and the earliest diamond-engraved glass objects seem to be of Venetian origin. Other countries, however, were not far behind, and Pastor Mathesius (no. 45) records in 1562 that people were "scratching all kinds of leafy scrollwork and beautiful flourishes with a diamond on the fine, smooth Venetian glass." He seems to have been thoroughly up-to-date, since the earliest-recorded glass with diamond-point engraving from northern or central Europe appears to be a tall, cylindrical *Stangenglas*, which is dated 1566 and is decorated with leafy scrolls and formal ornaments and bears the arms of the city of Vienna. A number of glasses of this kind exist, dating from this time well on into the seventeenth century and beyond, some of them attributable to centers such as Hall or Innsbruck, Nuremberg, etc.

The dish illustrated here is one of a set of six. All the others are decorated in the same way, with two coats-of-arms and six sprays of flowers and leaves, which may differ slightly from plate to plate. The arms are those of the Bohemian noble families of Schato von Schattenthal and von Berbisdorf. The "SSVS" of the plate was no doubt Severin Schato von Schattenthal, who was "Philosopher and Physician of the Kingdom of Bohemia"; the "MSSGB" was probably Margaretha von Berbisdorf, the date 1613 probably recording the date of their marriage.

The engraving of this dish shows well the firm and elegant outlines, with simple hatching, which were characteristic of this period.

Probably Bohemian,
dated 1613.
Height: 3.8 cm.
Gift of Edwin J. Beinecke

53

Dish with Diamond-point Engraving

The use of the diamond point for engraving on glass had been known in Venice as early as about 1535, and its special aptitude for decorating glass was exploited in various European countries during the second half of the sixteenth century, notably in Italy, Austria, Germany, Bohemia, England (no. 39), and the Netherlands. In the northern part of the latter country the art reached great heights in the second half of the seventeenth century (no. 54). Most of the "schools" of diamond-point engraving have a characteristic style that makes attribution possible within certain limits. The dish illustrated, however, does not fit exactly into any of these categories, although it is indisputably one of the great masterpieces in this genre. The use of a diamond point for engraving demands no prolonged training such as is necessary for the mastery of wheel engraving, and the basic desideratum is to be able to draw well. This is clearly a gift enjoyed by the artist of this dish, whose consummate mastery of line and unswerving firmness of touch is unsurpassed in the oeuvre of the best Dutch masters.

The monogram in the center of the dish has been interpreted as that of Gaston, Duc d'Orléans (1608–1660), son of Henri IV of France. The decoration of the rim consists of a series of panels surrounded by luxuriant wreaths of leaves and flowers that have attracted a selection of winged insects. The panels are alternately rectangular and oval, the former being left blank, the latter each enclosing an emblem. These emblems were enormously popular in the late sixteenth and seventeenth centuries, and some hundreds of books were published in this period illustrating them and explaining their symbolism. On the dish the emblem at the top is inscribed "ABRUM-PAM" ("I will cut off") and clearly refers to the precarious nature of temporal power, represented by the orb. That on the right proclaims "TESTANTE VIREBO" ("In bearing witness I shall flourish"—an obelisk wreathed with leaves); that on the bottom is inscribed "VERITAS PREMITUR NON OPPRIMITUR" ("Truth is concealed, not suppressed"—a book hidden in a palm tree). At the left is a sculptured bust on a pedestal, inscribed "CONCEDO NULLI" ("I yield to none"). In the *cavetto* of the dish the all-seeing eye of God shines from among the clouds, while cornucopias, symbolic of plenty, flank the initials on either side.

53
Probably French,
mid-17th century.
Height: 48.8 cm.
Endowment Fund Purchase

54

Serpent-stem Goblet with Diamond-point Engraving

A salient development in the *façon de Venise* glassmaking of the seventeenth century was an increasing complexity of stem treatment. Some of these stems were given three-dimensional forms, but a large number were apparently composed flat on the marver and then attached to the bowl and foot. Most of the stems of this type consist of a length of composite colored cane twisted into a figure eight or comparable shape. To the edges of this formation were added two strips of usually blue-green glass, the upper extremities of which were worked into the form of dragons' heads, the lower part being tooled and notched in a variety of designs. The total effect was of two coiled and intertwined serpents, and such glasses were referred to as *verres à serpents* in seventeenth-century documents relating to various glassmaking centers in the southern Netherlands, such as Liège, Brussels, Barbançon, and elsewhere. A number of these glasses bear inscriptions with dates in the seventies and eighties of that century—probably the heyday of this particular type of glass.

The Corning glass is diamond engraved with pairs of dancing or carousing peasants; below the rim runs a leafy scroll with flowers. This engraving is very close in style to that of a known Dutch engraver, Willem Mooleyser of Rotterdam. Seven glasses are known, dating between 1685 and 1697, which are signed by Mooleyser either in full or with his initials. Four of these, all dated either in 1685 or 1686, are engraved with peasant scenes closely comparable to those on the Corning goblet, the subject on at least one being taken from a print by Peter Nolpe (1613-14–1652-3).

Many other glasses, from as early as 1666, have been attributed to Mooleyser on grounds of style, but not all of these ascriptions are convincing, for there then must have been a number of engravers working in the same general style in the north Netherlands. This was a period when wheel engraving was beginning to establish itself in Holland, which may have influenced diamond-point engravers to work in scratched areas.

Probably Netherlandish,
c. 1670–85.
Height: 18.1 cm

124

56

Royal Covered Goblet

In 1676 a glasshouse was founded in Stockholm and later moved to Kungsholm, an island that formed the nucleus of the city. It was thereafter called the "Kungsholm glasshouse." The moving spirit in this undertaking was a certain Giacomo Bernardini Scapitta, originally a mendicant friar of Casale in the marquisate of Montferrat, in northwestern Italy. It is perhaps not without significance that the famous glassmaking center of Altare was also located within Montferrat, not far to the southwest of Casale. Despite his holy orders, Scapitta was an adventurer of considerable audacity, and while in Sweden he referred to himself as the Marquis Guagnini. He had apparently obtained some knowledge of glassmaking in Amsterdam, and in 1675 was able to convince the Swedish authorities of his talents in glassmaking by means of trials in an experimental furnace set up for the purpose in Stockholm. His success may have been due more to the skills of Jean Guillaume Reinier, who had accompanied him from Amsterdam, than to his own abilities. Scapitta's inability either to make glass or to run a glasshouse soon showed itself, however, and he fled to England in August 1678. The Kungsholm glasshouse continued production until 1815.

The Italian influence brought to Stockholm by Scapitta is perhaps to be detected in the covered goblet shown here. The elaborate stem echoes forms in *façon de Venise* glasses made elsewhere in northern Europe (no. 55). In the stem itself appear the initials C and E in a "mirror monogram"—the C for Carl XI, king of Sweden; the E for Ulrika Eleonora, the queen. Ulrika Eleonora was the sister of Christian V, king of Denmark, whom Carl XI had defeated at the Battle of Lund in 1676, the very year of the foundation of the Kungsholm glasshouse. The marriage was arranged as part of the settlement imposed on the northern powers by Louis XIV of France in 1679, and the Corning glass must date from some time between 1680 and Carl XI's death in 1697. Carl XI himself was interested in the progress of the Kungsholm glasshouse and indeed owned a share in it. It seems likely that this goblet, with its royal crown as cover finial and another crown above his initial and that of the queen, was a royal commission.

The goblet suffers from "glass disease" (crizzling), another common feature of northern glasses in the Venetian style (no. 55) and one very often found in Kungsholm glasses.

It is just possible that the goblet was made at a second glasshouse in Stockholm run by Gustav Jung between 1685 and his death in 1695, but the attribution to Kungsholm seems much more likely.

Swedish, Stockholm;
c. 1690.
Height (with cover): 46 cm

57

Diamond-engraved Bottle

Engraving with the diamond point in seventeenth-century Holland was not the preserve of the professional artist-decorator but a part of contemporary literature and culture. Its practitioners were cultivated amateurs often concerned more with literary pursuits than with the visual arts, and an essential point at which these interests converged was calligraphy. There were a considerable number of practitioners of the art who concentrated on inscriptions with literary overtones to the total exclusion of any form of representational or ornamental engraving, the most famous being Willem van Heemskerk, a cloth merchant of Leiden. For most of his long life he engraved glasses with literary tags in the most exquisite calligraphy, usually disposed around the body of a colored bottle in such a way that his letters and flourishes complemented and were complemented by the lettering on the other side of the glass. Van Heemskerk's inscriptions were usually in Dutch, but an earlier practitioner of the art, Anna Roemers Visscher, engraved Italian verses and employed Greek lettering on occasion. She, her sister Maria Tesselschade Roemers Visscher, and the somewhat younger Maria van Schurman, all glass engravers, were renowned bluestockings of their day, celebrated in verse by contemporary poets.

The Corning bottle is signed "B. Boers Warmond 20 April 1697." The artist has been identified as [Se]bastiaan Boers (d. 1713), described as a "French schoolmaster" at Warmond, not far from Leiden. In 1683 he appears to have owned the French boarding school there, which enjoyed a good reputation. The duties of a schoolmaster in those days included the teaching of fine handwriting, and evidently Bastiaan Boers excelled in this branch of his profession. The Corning bottle is inscribed in Dutch, as is a green bottle by Boers in the Rijksmuseum, Amsterdam. The text reads: "De vriendschap is's levens zout" ("Friendship is the salt of life"). A smaller inscription on the shoulder reads: "Helena Willem Zuyht(?)," presumably the name of an owner, and not necessarily written by Boers himself. The colorless glass and the slant-cut rim of this bottle are both unusual features.

Dutch,
dated 1697.
Height : 25.4 cm

131

58

Vase with Applied Decoration

Catalonia produced glass of Venetian inspiration in the sixteenth and seventeenth centuries, while farther south, in territory which for several hundred years had been Muslim, glass of a quite different character was made. In contrast to the more sophisticated decolorized glassware of northern and central Spain, the glass of the southeast was normally green or yellow, no special effort having been made to neutralize the colors produced by the iron impurities in the local sands. In this material glasses with a very strong Islamic flavor were made. The shape of the glass shown here is distinctly reminiscent of the mosque lamp form (no. 33), and the trumpet neck is a recurring feature of Islamic glassmaking. An echo of Near Eastern technique also may be detected in the profusion of applied ornament, which is characteristic of the southern Spanish glasses. The upper part of the neck and the lower part of the almost spherical body of this vase are encircled by glass threads, the lower circuits being pincered together at intervals to produce a chain motif. Applied hollow-blown handles run from the neck to the shoulder and are themselves decorated with notched trails, recalling the Teutonic claw beakers (no. 22), although these "claws" do not communicate with the vessel itself through the wall. The notched trails themselves are drawn down from a tooled point of application below the rim of the neck, and the foot has been tooled with diagonal impressions reminiscent of the finish of the feet in late Roman Egyptian glasses.

A number of centers are recorded in the provinces of Granada, Almería, and Jaen, notable among them being Castril de la Peña in Granada and María in Almería, where the Corning glass may have been made.

These green glasses were probably little regarded in their own day, and they do not appear in inventories in the same way as do the more highly prized "crystal" glasses of Catalonia and Cadalso. It was only toward the end of the nineteenth century that their originality and aesthetic merits came to be properly appreciated.

Spanish, probably Andalusia;
16th or 17th century.
Height: 14.9 cm

59

Wheel-engraved Crystal Plaque

With the breakdown of the Roman Empire in the west, the art of glass engraving was lost to northern Europe. The skill of engraving hardstones, however, probably never wholly died out, since the need to have signet rings for authenticating documents was ever present. In the late Middle Ages hardstone engraving grew greatly in importance and extended to the working of larger stones, from which could be formed cups, dishes, and so forth, for religious or secular use. By the sixteenth century workers had developed the skills to shape vessels of considerable size and to engrave them in intaglio with a variety of ornaments of great sophistication. It was from this stock of expertise that the art of glass engraving arose, as it undoubtedly had done in antiquity, and it is clearly from the equipment of the gem engraver that the glass engraver's wheel had its origins.

The first artist who exemplified this transposition was Caspar Lehmann, who from 1588 onward worked in Prague. In 1601 he was appointed by Emperor Rudolf II as the "Imperial Gem Engraver." From 1606–8 he worked for the elector of Saxony in Dresden, but in the latter year he was back in Prague with the title "Imperial Gem Engraver and Glass Engraver," a significant change. In fact, a glass beaker signed by him is dated 1605, and he was already engraving glass plaques during his stay in Dresden. In 1609 he was granted an imperial privilege allowing him alone to practice the art of glass engraving within the empire, since he had "discovered the art and business of glass engraving. . . ."

Lehmann died in 1622, and his privilege was inherited by his pupil Georg Schwanhardt, who moved to his native city of Nuremberg and founded a dynasty of glass engravers. Schwanhardt was for long regarded as having introduced the art to that city, which in the seventeenth century was the leading German center of glass engraving. However, a seventeenth-century source that had been overlooked stated that "Hans Wessler, a goldsmith, was the first to bring glass engraving to Nuremberg." As early as 1613 Wessler was referred to in an official document as "glass engraver" and ordered to forego his privilege as such for a term of twelve years. No work attributable to Wessler, however, had been identified until the plaque illustrated here was shown in 1958 in an international exhibition of glass in Liège. It is initialed "HW" and may safely be regarded as Wessler's work.

German, Nuremberg;
c. 1610–20.
Height: 15.3 cm.
Width: 11.5 cm

The plaque is copied from an engraving by the Nuremberg artist Georg Pencz (c. 1500–1550) and shows Tomyris, queen of the Messagetae, cutting off the head of the dead Cyrus, king of the Persians, who had invaded her kingdom and killed her son. The plaque betrays by its uncertain handling of perspective and modeling its status as one of the incunabula of the wheel engraver's art.

60

Goblet with Wheel-engraved Decoration

For the last three-quarters of the seventeenth century Nuremberg was the most important center of the wheel engraver's art in the whole of central Europe. On Caspar Lehmann's death, Georg Schwanhardt, who had inherited Lehmann's exclusive privilege to exercise the craft of wheel engraving (no. 59), returned to his native Nuremberg and there began a long series of engravings on both glass and rock crystal which display the most refined technique and fastidious taste. He was a master of figural engraving and executed delicate landscapes with infinitely varied renderings of tree foliage, often achieved in part by using the diamond point. With these elements he combined strong decorative scrollwork. The technique of polishing parts of the engraved area to give variety was attributed to him by contemporary writers.

Schwanhardt taught his art to his children: Heinrich, Georg, Sophia, Susanna, and Maria. Even the maid in this remarkable household learned to engrave glass. The younger Georg Schwanhardt was prevented from perfecting his art by a disease of the joints, and no glass of his is known. His brother Heinrich did not sign his glasses, and only one goblet can definitely be attributed to him on literary evidence. One contemporary historian of the arts in Nuremberg wrote that Heinrich Schwanhardt surpassed his father and excelled in calligraphy; the only goblet certainly attributable to Heinrich has in fact a long inscription in polished capitals on a matt ground. Some other glasses can be reasonably attributed to him, but there is great uncertainty in this field. A number of other glass engravers are known to have been active in Nuremberg at this time, and the work of a few of them is identifiable by means of signed glasses; to others it is not possible to attribute a single glass. One of Heinrich Schwanhardt's contemporaries (and particular *bête noire*) was Hermann Schwinger, who died in 1683 of consumption, aged forty-three. Fortunately, a number of his glasses are signed, and it is possible to form some idea of his style. He excelled in figural engraving (although Schwanhardt said that Schwinger could not draw and got others to do his designs for him), landscapes with buildings, coats-of-arms, and calligraphy. This versatility and skill must have been at the root of Schwanhardt's jealous hostility.

The goblet shown here, signed "Herman Schwinger" in diamond point on the bowl, is a certain work of Schwinger. This wheel-engraved goblet has the coats-of-arms of two Nuremberg patrician families, Fürer von Haimendorf (accompanied by the initials "HCF"), and Rieter von Kornburg ("H.P.A.R."); between these are two groups of military trophies. The linked coats-of-arms no doubt record a betrothal or marriage, the suitor-bridegroom being Paul Albrecht Rieter von Kornburg (1635–1704), who filled a number of high offices in the city of Nuremberg. This glass exemplifies a type of goblet found almost exclusively with Nuremberg engraving. Forming the stem is an elaborate succession of knops and interposed discs above a hollow-blown inverted baluster, and this formation is echoed in the finial of the cover (when present). It is not known where the glasses were made, and there is no evidence for glassmaking in Nuremberg itself at this date.

Germany, Nuremberg;
c. 1675–80.
Height: 31 cm.
Bequest of Jerome Strauss

61

Covered Goblet Engraved in Relief (Hochschnitt)

As the history of Caspar Lehmann shows (no. 59), the art of glass engraving grew from that of hardstone engraving during the sixteenth century; the heartland of this development was Prague, then capital of the Holy Roman Empire. Emperor Rudolf II was an impassioned collector of precious and semiprecious stones, and under his aegis there grew an entire organization, inside Bohemia and abroad, devoted to the collecting of suitable raw materials and to the setting-up of workshops where the stones could be carved and then suitably mounted in goldsmith's work. The energy required to reduce great blocks of rock crystal and other stones to the necessary shapes and to hollow them out was prodigious. At first energy was produced by the use of great wheels turned by hand, but by the end of the 1580s a water-powered mill for hardstone engraving had been installed on the banks of the Moldau River at Bubeneč, near Prague. When this did not suffice, a second mill was erected at Brandys on the Elbe River. Although the death of Rudolf II (1612) and the Thirty Years' War (1618–48) put an end to these grandiose projects, the Miseroni family of hardstone engravers continued in Prague throughout the war and until the death of Ferdinand Eusebio Miseroni in 1684. It was probably from the reservoir of talent available in this center of wheel engraving that the great expansion of Bohemian glass engraving in the second half of the seventeenth century drew its strength.

In 1685 Friedrich Winter was appointed glass engraver to Count Christoph Leopold Schaffgotsch, and it was no doubt at his insistence that the count installed at Hermsdorf (in the Hirschberger Tal, Silesia) a water-powered cutting shop for both glass and hardstones. This was not fully ready until 1690–1, but by this date Winter had ten to twelve glass engravers working for him at Hermsdorf. There are a number of glasses engraved in high relief with the Schaffgotsch arms, the ground of the glass having been cut back to achieve this, and there can be no doubt that they were made at the Hermsdorf workshop. The armorial emblems are characteristically accompanied by acanthus leaf motifs.

The glass illustrated here is engraved in this way, the acanthus leaf motif predominating in the decoration. On the bowl of the goblet, however, is engraved the portrait of Augustus II ("the Strong"), elector of Saxony and king of Poland (1670–1733), and on the cover his mirror monogram "AR" (for Augustus Rex). Although having strong affinity with the Schaffgotsch glasses, the goblet seems more likely to have been made at Potsdam and engraved in Berlin (no. 62) as a gift for Augustus—other examples are known. On the other hand, the goblet may have been made at Dresden, the Saxon capital, where relief engraving was certainly practiced and where by 1700 a house making crystal glass of fine quality for the court had been set up.

German, Potsdam or Dresden;
c. 1700.
Height: 34.3 cm

139

62

Covered Beaker Engraved in Intaglio and Relief

At the beginning of 1687 Martin Winter, glass engraver to the elector of Brandenburg, memorialized his master in Berlin in these somewhat ungrammatical terms: "Your Electoral Highness will graciously remember how not long since I humbly mentioned to you the matter of a cutting mill; if now your Electoral Highness entertains the gracious desire to have something especially of raised work, and to work up such from the rough without water power is very hard and tedious; on the other hand, if this cutting mill were set to work, one would be able to make something good and fine much more easily and quickly. . . ." Winter had already done engraving in relief for the elector in 1683 and knew what he was talking about. Moreover, he was the brother of Friedrich Winter, the engraver who worked for Count Schaffgotsch at Hermsdorf (no. 61) and who was undoubtedly responsible for the erection of a water-powered cutting shop there. Martin Winter got his way, and orders were given in 1687 for the erection of the mill. It may be presumed that this signaled the beginning of relief engraving (*Hochschnitt*) on a large scale in Berlin.

In 1680 Martin Winter was installed as glass engraver to the elector of Brandenburg and brought with him his nephew, named Gottfried Spiller, who had worked as his apprentice since 1675. In 1683 Spiller was taken on strength as "journeyman glass engraver" with a salary of two hundred thaler (Winter got five hundred), and on Winter's death in 1702 he succeeded to his uncle's title. Spiller was well-enough known in his time to be mentioned in several contemporary works on the arts in Berlin. Thanks to a description in one of these, it is possible to attribute one glass to him with reasonable certainty, and one signed rock crystal is known. On the evidence of these pieces it is possible in turn to attribute a considerable number of glasses to his hand, among them some of the most exquisite engravings in the history of the art, cut with a sureness of touch and a delicacy that are second to none. All this work is in intaglio, partly matt, partly polished, but it is almost invariably accompanied by borders in relief that perhaps may have been executed by others among the considerable number of engravers working in the Berlin atelier by the River Spree. Before his death in 1702, some of this work may have been done by Martin Winter himself, though it has not proved possible to distinguish between his style and his nephew's.

The goblets and beakers, sometimes in crystal, sometimes in ruby glass, engraved in the Berlin cutting shop were made in the neighboring Potsdam glasshouse, which also directly served the elector of Brandenburg. The present glass bears on the front the mirror monogram of the Elector Frederick III of Brandenburg—"F.C.B." (for "Fredericus Churfürst [zu] Brandenburg") in an oval panel surmounted by the electoral crown. On the reverse is a similar panel enclosing the Brandenburg coat-of-arms. The series of deeply cut relief borders and the sculptured finial are characteristic of the *Hochschnitt* work done in the Berlin workshop.

German, Potsdam (glass)
and Berlin (engraving);
c. 1690–1700.
Height (with cover): 21.9 cm.
Gift of Edwin J. Beinecke

63

Lead-glass Roemer

From the time when clear, colorless glass first became familiar in England, in the sixteenth century, Venetian-style *cristallo* had been the most coveted and imitated type of glass. Yet it was far from having the quality of natural crystal, being usually of a brownish or grayish tone, and from the middle of the seventeenth century onward there was a quiet drift of taste away from the ideal represented by the Venetian glass. Not only were glassmakers anxious to obtain an absolutely colorless material, but there was a reaction against the brittle thinness of Venetian glass. The glass industry, disrupted by the civil war in England (1642–51), had been recovering since the Restoration of Charles II in 1660, and in that very year a certain John de la Cam undertook to make "Cristall de roach" in a glasshouse in London. No glass attributable to this factory is known, and for a number of years the London glass sellers continued to obtain supplies from Venice, considering them still to be the best available. One of them, John Greene, writing to his Venetian supplier in November 1672, stipulated that the glasses should be "of verij good cleer whit sound Mettall; for trulj the last you sent me the Mettall was indifferent good and cleer, but not so sound and strong as theij should have bin made; for therin Lies the excelencj of your Venetian glasses that they are generallij stronger than ours made heer. . . ." Two years later, however, the Venetian ambassador was writing home of "the extreme beauty of the English drinking glasses. They are very white and thick, in imitation of rock crystal, but very far from real perfection . . . they are soft, fragile and extremely dear. . . ."

In March 1674, George Ravenscroft applied to the crown for a patent for "a particular sort of Christalline glass," and in April he signed an agreement with the influential Company of Glass Sellers to sell to them alone his next three years' output. Unfortunately for both parties, the new colorless glass suffered from a constitutional imbalance that produced the defect then known as crizzling, in which a surface roughening is accompanied by a network of glistening internal cracks. Ravenscroft was forced to revise his formula, and this he did by adding increasing doses of lead oxide to his batch, a revolutionary idea. By about the middle of 1676 the crizzling defect was thought to be overcome, and in October of that year it was announced that the improved glasses were to be marked with a seal. In due course this was stamped with a raven's head, taken from the Ravenscroft coat-of-arms. This marks the beginning of the great tradition of lead glass in England.

The Corning glass illustrated here is one of three known *Roemers* (no. 48) marked with the seal. All are different and of differing sizes. The largest has gadrooning around the base of an otherwise plain bowl. It is diamond engraved with scenes relating to a visit to Danzig by the king of Poland in 1677–78. The second, like the glass here, is decorated with vertical mold-blown ribbing on bowl and foot, but on the Corning example this has been pinched laterally to form a mesh design—"nipt diamond waies," in the jargon of Ravenscroft's own price list of 1677. Curiously enough, the *Roemer* shape is not obviously referred to in this list. The shape, however, continued in sporadic use in England right into the eighteenth century.

English, London;
c. 1676–77.
Height: approx. 18.8 cm

64

Baluster Goblet of Lead Glass

The "glass of lead" invented by George Ravenscroft (no. 63) was soon copied by other English glassmakers (and in some instances by those on the Continent who profited by the knowledge of absconding workmen). Gradually the ratio of lead in the mixture was increased until it reached a level of about 33 percent of the total batch. Although for centuries lead had been known as a constituent of various enamel glasses, the new lead crystal was essentially a material that glassmen had never before in history blown and worked. Its working properties were different from those of Venetian-type *cristallo*, the glass remaining longer in a workable condition and therefore requiring less instant dexterity than was needed to achieve the pastry-cook effects of the best Venetian gaffers. It was also incapable of being worked into some of the sharper and more complex forms that were the stock-in-trade of the most skilled seventeenth-century continental masters. In England toward the end of the century elaborate goblets with figure-eight stems and crown finials were made; these seem more ponderous than their continental counterparts. During the last quarter of the seventeenth century, however, the English glassmakers developed a style of their own that to some extent harked back to the relatively simple shapes desired by John Greene from his Venetian supplier, Allesio Morelli. In the latest of the drawings sent to Venice, a change of emphasis is apparent, with mainly round-funnel bowls mounted on baluster or "inverted baluster" stems, sometimes shown as being four-lobed in section. For these simple shapes the new lead glass was ideal. Its clarity and capacity to hold the light were shown to best advantage in plain undecorated bowls (although occasionally an enclosed air bubble in the base showed off the light-refracting quality of the glass), while a variety of stem formations, all circular in cross section, provided the vehicle for an alternation of deep shade and brilliant light such as had never been seen in glass before. The variety of these stem forms is potentially infinite and in practice is bewildering. The glass shown here has, in collector's jargon, an angular knop above a small basal knop, through both of which runs a tear caught in the moment of hardening as if it were ascending through an oily medium. The round-funnel bowl above and the domed foot with wide fold below complete a balanced composition, the repose of which is enlivened by an infinitely varied play of light and shade.

English,
early 18th century.
Height: 24.7 cm

65

Wheel-engraved Hookah Base

One of the European commodities that found a good sale in the Far East in the seventeenth and eighteenth centuries was glass. Neither India nor China (no. 82) had a strong tradition of indigenous glassmaking, least of all in the field of blown glass, and the superior quality of European glass made it a favored export. With the ascendancy of the English East India Company on the Indian subcontinent, there was a great increase in English imports, both for the use of English residents and for sale to the native population. Shortly after 1721, for example, five chests of glassware, one chest of "Perspective Glasses" (telescopes), and thirteen chests of looking glasses formed part of an outward consignment valued at nearly five hundred pounds, a considerable sum at that time. An advertisement of 1737 records the export of more than six thousand pieces of glass. Much of this may have been purely utilitarian, but an early eighteenth-century East India Company document records "Comon Glass ware sold at 1 Rupee per lb. and ffine as Hubbubbells etc. from 4 Rs to 5 Rs per lb." "Hubbubbell" was a version of the word "hubble-bubble," later in the eighteenth century called "the poor man's hookah" by the German traveler Carsten Niebuhr. The hookah was a waterpipe in which the tobacco smoke was sucked through scented water to free it of its noxious or harsh qualities, the bubbling sound of this no doubt suggesting the name "hubble-bubble." This term was employed in the company records as early as 1694 in a letter referring to gifts which were to be sent to India: " . . . in the latter is included the p[ar]ticular presents that I think needfull to be sent the huble bubles and Glass wares must be bespoake according to the p[ar]ticulars inclosed rec[eive]d from Bengall . . ."; four hubble-bubbles are recorded as having been sent to Ceylon in 1696.

There is ample evidence, therefore, for the export of hookah bases from England to India, and the high-quality glass, probably containing lead, of the piece here confirms the distinction made in the company document recording glass prices, quoted above. This suggests that the hookah itself is of English rather than Indian origin. It has evidently, however, been locally wheel engraved, probably in Delhi, for this work agrees both in technique and in style with the engraving on jade and rock crystal long recognized as being made for the Moghul court. A very similar pipe base with a light lead content is relief engraved in arabic script with the formula: "In the name of God the Clement, the merciful . . ." etc., and with verses invoking the good fellowship of the hookah.

Tobacco smoking appears to have reached India toward the end of the reign of the great Moghul Emperor Akbar (1556–1605). To be used for smoking, the hookah base would have to be filled with scented water into which passed a tube connected with a cup containing the tobacco on glowing charcoal. A second tube passing through a disc sealing the orifice of the hookah base was used to suck the smoke through the water.

English (glass)
and Indian (engraving),
late 17th century.
Height: 19.6 cm

66

Wheel-engraved Covered Goblet with Decorative Threads

Potash-lime glass of reasonable clarity had been made in Bohemia probably before 1600 and had been the vehicle of some of the earliest wheel engraving on glass (no. 59). Although glassmaking continued in parts of Bohemia during the Thirty Years' War, the upheavals due to the war seriously disrupted industry and commercial life in most parts of the kingdom. With the Peace of Westphalia in 1648 great efforts were made to restore the economic life of the country, and one of the favored methods was the establishing of glasshouses on the great estates that abounded in woodlands to produce the fuel needed. At the same time, efforts were clearly made in a number of centers to improve the quality of the glass produced. A book of 1679 refers to glass "which in transparency and brilliance came near to crystal" made in a glasshouse of the Count Kaunitz near Falkenau. By this date, however, the glassworks had already closed, and in 1686 an important glass dealer, himself an engraver, could complain that no glass of good quality could be obtained in this area, so he had to obtain his from the Schreiberhau district on the Silesian side of the Riesengebirge range.

The technical solution to the problem of obtaining a solid and colorless "crystal" glass was to use chalk or lime added deliberately to the batch. The first mention of this type of glass comes from southern Bohemia, where Michael Müller developed the technique at the Helmbach glasshouse, not far from Budweis, in about 1683. In his treatise *Ars Vitraria Experimentalis,* Johann Kunckel, the manager and technician of the Potsdam factory, merely hinted at an improved formula in the first edition of 1679; in the second edition of 1689 he openly gives two recipes involving the addition of a considerable ratio of chalk to the batch. By 1700 this improved glass, especially suitable for wheel engraving, had become standard throughout Bohemia and was already making a name for itself abroad.

The necessary skill to engrave the glasses was also freely available, particularly in northeastern Bohemia and in Silesia, on the northern side of the mountains (no. 67). The goblet illustrated here is certainly of Bohemian origin, its stem and cover finial being decorated with twisted threads of ruby glass, a Bohemian specialty. It is possible, however, that its decoration was carried out in Silesia, for it shows a view of the city of Oels, some distance to the east of Breslau (the modern Wroclaw), the chief city in Silesia. Views of cities, however, were often engraved in Bohemia itself, and it is impossible to be sure on which side of the mountains this goblet was decorated.

*Bohemian,
c. 1710–20.
Height (with
cover): 26.7 cm*

67

Covered Goblet with Wheel-cut and -engraved Decoration

The distinction between where a glass was made and where it was decorated (no. 66) can be observed in the Silesian-engraved glasses of the eighteenth century. There were a number of engraving workshops active in this area, but only one signed glass survives—a goblet inscribed "Caspar Gottlieb Langer in Warmbrunn Glasschneider 1749." Warmbrunn was certainly one of the most important of these centers; as a bathing resort it offered mementos to the visitor, a practice that was to become even more popular in the nineteenth century. In 1733 there were six glass engravers working there, and by 1743 this number had risen to more than forty. The names of a number of them are known, but they cannot be associated with any particular glasses. One of them, however, and fortunately probably the most accomplished, left behind him a number of pulls made from his own glasses by means of wetted paper. These have made it possible to establish some notion of his work and his style. His name was Christian Gottfried Schneider (1710–1773), and it is evident that he was a consummate master in rendering with the engraving wheel the most elaborate rococo scrollwork and other ornaments, which he appears to have been able to work up with the utmost ease and fluency. His figural engraving was less sure, and he was not a good draftsman. Frequently, therefore, if not always, he used a print as the basis for this kind of work, improvising the background to suit his own taste.

The covered goblet illustrated here takes its place with at least three other goblets with the same theme of decoration—a pair of lovers in a park setting, a little girl behind them holding up a garland of flowers. These glasses can be safely attributed to Schneider by reference to one of the pulls referred to above (now in the Museum of Jelenia Góra, Poland). The Corning glass differs from the pull only in a somewhat sparser setting of trees and scrollwork, no doubt because the space is restricted on either side by the relief-cut scrolls. This relief cutting itself is a reminder of the earlier relief work of Friedrich Winter and others in Hermsdorf, which was not far away and which, like Warmbrunn, formed a part of the estates of the Counts Schaffgotsch (no. 61).

The shape of this goblet, with the base of its bowl forming a concave curve, is typical of the Silesian glasses of the period about 1760, and the glass was no doubt made in one of the glasshouses of the Hirschberger Tal. Before it was ready for the engraver, it had been worked over by the cutter, who would have faceted the stem, the base of the bowl, and the underside of the foot, and probably cut most of the relief work.

Silesian,
c. 1760–70.
Height (with
cover): 28 cm

68

Wheel-engraved Goblet and Cover

Wheel engraving appears to have started in the Netherlands in the 1650s, where it was practiced concurrently with the more popular diamond-point engraving (no. 54). The late seventeenth-century Dutch wheel engraving was of no particular distinction, but in the next century a number of engravers brought the art to a high pitch of excellence. Preeminent among them was Jacob Sang of Amsterdam, who was certainly related to Andreas Friedrich Sang, court engraver at Weimar, and to Johann Heinrich Balthasar Sang, who held a similar post at Brunswick. Indeed, in an advertisement Jacob Sang called himself "a Saxon artist-glass-engraver." Much of Sang's engraving was executed on English glasses, of which there was a considerable export to Holland toward the middle years of the century—so much so that in 1750 the Amsterdam guild of glass- and earthenware-sellers had to seek permission to include the handling of English glass and pottery within the articles of its regulations. No doubt the soft lead crystal, with its subdued brilliance, was considered a sympathetic material for the engraver's art.

The engraver of the goblet illustrated here presumably shared the predilection for English glass. It is signed "W : O : R. FECIT," and these initials may safely be identified as those of Willem Otto Robart, born at The Hague in 1696. Three other signed glasses by this engraver bear the dates 1735, 1743, and 1778, respectively.

The goblet is elaborately embellished with four coats-of-arms in scrolled cartouches, all interlinked. One of these is inscribed "C:E:Van Derlith," associating it with Charlotte Elisabeth van der Lith (b.1700), daughter of a clergyman of the Dutch Reformed Church, who in 1722 went to the then Dutch colony of Surinam in the East Indies. There in 1725 she married Hendrik Temming, the governor, whose arms are to the left on the glass. Temming died in 1727, and two years later she married his successor, Charles Emilius Henry, Marquis de Cheusses, whose arms are to the right of the group. He died in 1734, and in 1737 she married Governor Joan Raye, who died in the same year. His arms are at the bottom of the glass. The long Latin inscription on the reverse celebrates, not without justice, this "distinguished widow of three Governors of Surinam. . . ." Engraved on the cover are three children with a cornucopia playing in the rays of the sun and accompanied by the inscription (in Latin): "Thrice wife, and mother of three, now widowed, she governs her offspring and enlightens her family." The dedication seems to be the work of an admirer, and in 1742, a year after the date of the goblet, this lady married yet again, this time a clergyman who had come out to the colony—he died in 1744; in 1748 she married yet another clergyman, also fated not to succeed her, dying in 1751. She herself, having outlived five husbands in the space of twenty-six years, died in 1753.

English (glass) and Dutch (engraving), dated 1741. Height (with cover): 43.8 cm

Diamond-stippled Wineglass

Frans Greenwood was born April 17, 1680, in Rotterdam, of English descent. He married Maria van den Hoolaart in or before 1719, in which year she died. In 1726 he went into the civil service in Dordrecht, where he died in 1761. Frans Greenwood is a good example of the literary and artistic dilettante who made a specialty of glass engraving with the diamond point. In this he was in the true line of descent of such seventeenth-century amateurs as Anna Roemers Visscher and Willem van Heemskerk (no. 57). His son Cornelis was a painter; G.H. Hoolaart, another diamond-point engraver, was probably his nephew. He himself was a *littérateur*, publishing in 1719 a book of poems dedicated to Jacob Zeeus, who had dedicated two manuscript poems to him in 1714. He was probably a friend and certainly an acquaintance of Aert Schouman, also of Dordrecht but thirty years his junior, who painted and engraved Greenwood's portrait, and probably also reproduced this copper engraving in diamond stipple on a glass that survives. Schouman was also a member of the same artists' club as Greenwood's son Cornelis, and was not only a well-known painter and engraver in his own day, but also a distinguished practitioner of the diamond point on glass. These crossties between members of the literary and artistic coteries of eighteenth-century Holland could be multiplied more or less indefinitely. It is no coincidence that two of Greenwood's glasses, no doubt engraved after his own designs, are dedicated to "Poesis" ("Poetry") and "Pictura" ("Painting").

Frans Greenwood's special contribution to the art of diamond-point engraving was the use of stippling (making light dots with the diamond point), to the virtual exclusion of line engraving. His earliest-known glass, dated 1720 (when he was already forty years old), is executed entirely in line, but a wineglass in the Hessisches Landesmuseum in Cassel, dated 1722, is exclusively in stipple. At first his figures were drawn in isolation against the untouched ground of the glass, but later he stippled in the whole background, thus making it unnecessary to outline his subject against its ground. This technique was closely followed by Aert Schouman, and from Greenwood's time onward virtually all diamond-point engraving in Holland was done by the stipple method. Except for engravings probably after his own designs, such as those showing flowers, a lyre, or a palette ("Poetry" and "Painting" mentioned above), Greenwood normally closely followed engravings by or after artists such as Jan van Mieris, Arie de Vois, Paulus Moreelse, and others. The Corning glass no doubt followed some such model.

The actual glass on which Greenwood worked in this instance was probably English, as are most of those he used. The formation of its stem, however, is not altogether typical of English glasses at this period. There were a few glasshouses in the southern Netherlands making glass "in the English style" in the first half of the eighteenth century; at 's Hertogenbosch, in Holland itself, there was a factory making crystal glass, although it is not known just when it opened its doors.

England (glass)
and Dordrecht,
Holland (engraving);
dated 1746.
Height: 25 cm

Spirit Flask with Wheel-engraved and Enameled-painted Decoration

One of the most original German innovations in glass decoration was the adoption of translucent stained-glass enamels for the embellishment of glass vessels. The probable originator of this form of decoration and certainly its most distinguished practitioner was Johann Schaper of Nuremberg (no. 49). Around him formed a small school of artists, including Johann Ludwig Faber, Abraham Helmhack, and Hermann Benckert, who worked at Frankfurt-am-Main. All these men, like Schaper, also enameled pottery (usually the contemporary tin-glazed wares made in Holland and Germany), and this dual competence was a hallmark of the outside decorators, or *Hausmaler*, as they were called in Germany. At the turn of the eighteenth century, Chinese porcelain became more common in the countries of central Europe, and this also was decorated with enamels, often in somewhat awkward juxtaposition with the underglaze blue decoration already on the wares when they arrived in Europe. This work was executed mainly in Austria and Bohemia, rather than in Germany, and among its earliest and best-known practitioners were members of the Preissler family, notably Daniel (1636–1733) and his son Ignaz (1676–1741). It is noteworthy that the father is recorded as having brought the use of black and red enamels from "Holland" into Bohemia.

Ignaz Preissler was born in Friedrichswalde in Silesia. His main occupation seems to have been as *Hausmaler* to Count Franz Karl Liebsteinsky von Kolowrat at Reichenau Castle, in Kronstadt, Bohemia. It seems possible that his father was similarly employed there, perhaps as early as 1680. Apart from his work on porcelain, Ignaz Preissler certainly decorated glass, and a surviving dish decorated in the manner usually attributed to him—with black enamel and gilding—bears the arms of von Kolowrat. The Corning spirit flask is painted not only in the black and red enamels already referred to, but also with touches of purple, a color that appears on some of his early porcelains, sometimes used alone in a monochrome scheme of decoration. The flask was originally paired with another decorated in the same way (now in the Berlin Museum) and probably belonged to a set contained in a traveling case. Apart from its enameled decoration, it is wheel engraved with the arms of the Loēn family of Anhalt. The figure of the youthful Bacchus, derived from a print by Jost Amman (1539–1591), sets the tone for the decoration of the two flasks, made explicit in the accompanying inscription: "More Palatino bibimus ne Gutta supersit/ unde Suam possit Musca levare Sitim" ("We drink in the Palatine way so that not a drop is left from which a fly could quench his thirst"). The companion flask has a representation of men and women eating and drinking, with the inscription, "Thus it was in the days of Noah," and with another inscription in praise of food and drink.

Bohemian,
c. 1720–30.
Height: 20.9 cm

71

Pair of Enameled and Gilt Goblets

In Germany, from the second half of the sixteenth century onward, enameling was used as a means of decorating transparent, colorless glass (no. 46), but the idea seems to have been alien in England until the middle of the eighteenth century, a time when the production of enamels painted on copper became of commercial importance, especially in the Midlands, in Birmingham and other centers nearby. The opaque white ground of enamel on copper was in appearance much like porcelain, which had been imitated in opaque white glass in England since before 1700. It was therefore but a step to transfer enamel-painted decoration, common to both porcelain and enamels on metal, to opaque white glass. Numerous examples of English enameled opaque white glass are known.

It was not until at least a decade after this development, however, that the idea of enameling transparent, colorless glass was adopted. This innovation seems to stand to the credit of a family of craftsmen named Beilby, whose home was in Newcastle-upon-Tyne. Glassmaking had been practiced there for more than a century, and lead glass of excellent quality was being manufactured before the middle of the eighteenth century. Apart from the fact that a number of the enameled glasses are signed "Beilby," a good deal is known about the Beilbys because of the coincidence that the great wood engraver Thomas Bewick (1753–1828) was apprenticed in 1767 to one of the brothers, Ralph Beilby. Bewick records in his *Memoir* of his own life that Ralph was the fourth son of William Beilby, senior, who "had followed the business of a goldsmith and jeweller in Durham, where he was greatly respected. He had taken care to give all his family a good education. His eldest son, Richard, had served his apprenticeship to a die-sinker, or seal-engraver, in Birmingham. His second son, William, had learned enameling and painting in the same place. The former of these had taught my master seal-cutting, and the latter taught his brother Thomas and his sister, Mary enameling. . . ." Thomas (b. 1747) was seven years younger than William and by 1769 had moved to Leeds as a drawing master; and whereas Bewick records that Ralph Beilby "had also assisted his brother and sister in their constant employment of enamel painting on glass," he was an exceptionally busy engraver who rarely turned down work. It seems unlikely, therefore, that much of the Beilbys's enameling was done by either of these two brothers.

It is evident that William was the leading enameler, with Mary (nine years younger) perhaps as his helper. William was apprenticed in 1755 to a drawing master and enameler of Birmingham named John Haseldine, and his first glasses were probably painted the year he was free of his apprenticeship, in 1762. A decanter is known with this date scratched on it with a diamond, and the goblets painted with the royal arms and the Prince of Wales's feathers, probably celebrating the birth of the future George IV, were no doubt painted in the same year or very shortly afterward. It is noteworthy that these include the only two known glasses signed with the initial "W. Beilby," making his authorship explicit. A number of other glasses are signed "Beilby J[unio]r," and must have been painted before his father's death in 1765. The Corning goblets illustrated are signed merely "Beilby Invᵗ & pinxᵗ." They bear the arms, crest, and motto of the earls of Pembroke and Montgomery, and were no doubt made for Henry, the tenth earl (b. 1734). Two other virtually identical goblets are known, and the four originally may have formed part of a set of half-a-dozen. Apart from the heraldic decoration, they illustrate admirably the mantling and delicate pendant swags of leaves and flowers in white enamel that are an invariable accompaniment of the other forms of decoration on the Beilby glasses and are sometimes their sole ornament.

English,
Newcastle-upon-Tyne; c. 1765–70.
Height: 22.3 cm

72

Bottle and Two Tumblers of Enameled Opaque White Glass

Opaque white glass had been made in Venice since the middle of the fourteenth century, and in the late fifteenth and early sixteenth centuries it was used as a base for enameling and gilding (no. 35). Its use for the making of vessels then was no doubt inspired by the Chinese porcelain that reached Venice in quantities denied to northern Europe until about 1600. By the late seventeenth century the idea of imitating porcelain in opaque white glass had caught on in France, Germany, and England, and in the next century it was taken up again in Venice with renewed interest, despite (or perhaps because of) the introduction of porcelain manufacture into Venetian territory from about 1720 onward.

We are fortunately in a position to be virtually certain who made these eighteenth-century Venetian opaque white glasses. In the Victoria and Albert Museum in London there is a *lattimo* dish painted, in the same colors as the Corning pieces, with the figure of a parrot seated on a perch. Around this central theme and around the rim of the dish run borders of similar character to those decorating the neck of the Corning flask; to the parrot's right are painted flowers identical to those on the middle spray to the left of the parrot on the Corning piece. The London dish is marked "Al Giesù Murano" ("At the Sign of Jesus"), and it is known that the glasshouse bearing this name was owned and run by the Miotti family, ancient Muranese glassmakers. They are known to have made opaque white glass in slab form for the use of enamelers, so it may reasonably be assumed that the glasses described here were made as well as decorated in their glasshouse. The flowers of the Corning bottle recur in the form of a running floral scroll on the London dish, and this feature is found again on a smaller dish in the Cecil Higgins Art Gallery, at Bedford, England, which also has the formal border design. The center of this dish is painted with a peacock sitting on sprays of flowers and strawberries, exactly like the birds on the Corning tumblers; on a comparable plate in the museum at Coburg, Germany, the bird represented is a goldfinch, as on the right-hand tumbler in the illustration here.

The same choice of flowers, in the same colors, is found again in the corner motifs on two *lattimo* plaques in the Murano Museum, one painted with "Cain slaying Abel," the other with "Joseph and Potiphar's Wife." These plaques are inscribed "Al Gesù Murano 1731," thus giving us a date for this type of work.

The Corning flask is mounted in a way that suggests its use was as a perfume sprinkler intended for the oriental market. In the seventeenth and eighteenth centuries Venetian glassmaking was subjected to intense competition from other European glass industries, and the Muranese made great efforts to retain the Near Eastern market.

Venetian (Miotti factory),
c. 1730–35.
Height: (bottle) 27.5 cm;
(tumblers) 8.75 cm (left);
8.6 cm (right)

160

Verre de Nevers Lampworked Figure

The technique of building up small objects from rods and tubes of glass melted in a localized flame probably dates back to antiquity. Head beads apparently made in this way (although it is possible that at this date such objects were made at the furnace itself) date back as early as the fifth and fourth centuries B.C. There is no evidence of an unbroken tradition in this art through the Roman period and the Dark Ages, and traces of it are picked up again only in the fifteenth century. In the *Mémoires d'Olivier de la Marche* (1454) there is a description of a table ornament at a banquet given in the castle of Lille, allegedly made by a glassmaker of that town; it consisted of "a very beautiful fountain partly in glass and partly in lead of a very new aspect, for there were small trees made of glass, with marvelous leaves and flowers; and in . . . a clearing, surrounded by rocks there was a small St. Andrew. . . . " It seems certain that the trees and the figure of St. Andrew were made "at the lamp." The craft probably continued in unbroken succession in France from this point onward.

Some time between 1565 and 1577 *émailleurs* (enamelers) who made figures appeared at Nevers, in central France. At this period the rulers of Nevers were the Italian dukes of Mantua, and they encouraged Italian craftsmen to work in their dominions, among them glassmakers; it is possible that the lampworkers, too, were of Italian origin, the art then being well established in Italy. No examples of Nevers work dating to the sixteenth or even the seventeenth centuries are known, but it is recorded as early as 1605 that Louis XIII as a child played with "little glass dogs and other animals made at Nevers." A considerable number of lampworked "Nevers" figures are known from the eighteenth and nineteenth centuries, and the names of some of the artists are recorded.

Haudicquer de Blancourt in his *De l'art de la Verrerie* (1697) gives some description of the method of working of "those who make . . . divers human figures, animals of the earth, birds, vases and other curiosities . . . and all that by the sole heat of a lighted lamp; and a little metal tube which they use to blow this flame against the substance, which they get to melt quickly, forming of it such figures as they desire. . . ." Eighteenth-century engravings show three craftsmen seated at a table below which is a bellows distributing air under pressure to three nozzles in front of the workers. In front of them they have small, flat, oil-fed lamps waisted in shape like the sole of a shoe, with a wick projecting at the front. The flame from this was intensified by the bellows sufficiently to melt the glass rod, which was then manipulated with a pair of small tongs. Sometimes the figures were built up on metal armatures.

The Corning figure shows a beggar, perhaps an ex-soldier, of whom many must have been found on the streets during the war-troubled reign of Louis XV (1715–74).

French, probably Nevers; 18th century.
Height: 5.1 cm

Pair of Cut and Wrought Candlesticks

It is very difficult for modern man to imagine what life was like before the advent of gas and electricity supplied illumination at night. In northern Europe the candle was the normal means of lighting houses of any pretension. Candles were of two kinds: tallow, an admixture of animal fats, which was relatively cheap but smelly; or wax, usually beeswax but sometimes of vegetable origin, which was more expensive, comparatively odorless, and burned longer and more brightly with less attention. Wax candles were three times as expensive as tallow, and in England they attracted a tax eight times as heavy. Both types required snuffing at intervals—that is, the burned wick required trimming—but the tallow more frequently than the wax. Wax candles were therefore a symbol of social standing, and a major item of household expenditure. They were accordingly used sparingly, and the interiors of even great houses were extremely dim by modern standards. Queen Charlotte's dressing room in 1772 "being very large and hung with crimson damask, was very dark, there being only four candles. . . ." In well-ordered households it was normally only on festive occasions that the house was really brightly lit, as when in 1769 Lady Cowper "had an assembly in my great room, with above five dozen wax lights in the room."

The most opulent candlesticks were of silver, but English lead glass, on account of its light-refracting powers, provided an excellent substitute, particularly from the time when cutting became prevalent and exploited this particular quality of glass to the utmost. The earliest advertisement is Jerom Johnson's "FOR CUT GLASS" of 1742: ". . . the right and most curious Lustres, new fashioned Salts, Diamond-cut and scalloped Candlesticks. . . ." The pair illustrated, however, are tentatively cut; even the scalloped outline on the foot has only simple faceting. The candleholder is plain, and the stem alone is elaborately ornamented in a way that echoes the structure of its metal prototype. The main component, which gives the stick its height, is an eight-angled "Silesian" stem turned upside-down and sandwiched between two globular knops enclosing air bubbles; these components are separated by discs, and a composite swelling knop, seemingly built up of a number of discs, is interposed between this part of the stem and the foot. The reeded "Silesian" stem was in reality derived from German (probably Thuringian) glassmaking, and it is an elaboration of a four-sided stem introduced into England about 1710–15. At first employed for wineglasses (with the shoulder uppermost), its use was subsequently extended to sweetmeat glasses, salvers, and candlesticks, and lasted in these forms long after it had ceased to be used for drinking glasses.

Silver candlesticks were frequently made in sets of four, but this is not recorded in glassware. Indeed, an advertisement of 1755 records "several pair of cut-glass candlesticks in shagreen cases"; and when in 1722 General Hart rented a house on Nevis, in the West Indies, among the effects in the bedchamber were "two glass candlestick and a glass bell." Candlesticks seem not to have been unduly expensive, being recorded in 1746 at three shillings each for the best quality.

English, c. 1740.
Height: 25.75 cm (both)

Pair of Blue Cut-glass Bowls

The technical capacity to make blue transparent glass has hardly ever been beyond the resources of the glassmaker, and this was certainly true of the English glassmen of the eighteenth century. From the Ravenscroft period in the last quarter of the previous century (no. 63) at least one blue English glass has survived (the Savoy Vase in the Toledo Museum of Art). The fact that little blue glass exists that can be dated to the first half of the eighteenth century is almost certainly a matter of taste and not of inability to produce the color. This capacity, however, depended on a supply of cobalt in the form of smalt. Cobalt is an intensely potent coloring agent and had to be diluted first by fritting the cobalt ore with sand to produce a substance called "zaffer"; this in turn was diluted by fusing it with potassium carbonate to make a kind of blue glass that was itself reduced to powder form. This was smalt.

In the first half of the eighteenth century the country's needs for cobalt were met by imports from Saxony, where it was mined in the Schneeberg district. The amount imported increased by over 50 percent between 1747 and 1754, and some of this increase may well have been accounted for by the demand for blue glass. To counter the cost of imports, in 1754 the Royal Society of Arts offered a premium for the best sample of English cobalt; in the following year another premium was offered for the manufacture of zaffer and smalt from the native ore, which had in the meantime been identified in Cornwall. In 1756 Stephen More, secretary of the society, could write: "Some of this zaffre was given to Mr. Stephen Hall, partner with Mr. Hughes, Glass Maker, at the Faulkon Glass House, Southwark, who a few days later gave me a small piece of glass of a most excellent Blew Colour. . . ."

It is clear that although almost all eighteenth-century English blue glass is called "Bristol," the substance was in fact made in a number of centers. In 1751 a visitor to Stourbridge commented that glass was made there "in all the capital colours," and blue glass was advertised by the Warrington Warehouse in Lancashire in 1767 and by the New Glass Houses in Sunderland in 1769. It was certainly also made in Bristol as early as 1762. London, however, was probably the main producer, and certainly much blue glass with gilt decoration was manufactured there. In 1752 the *Birmingham Gazette* had advertised, "Just arrived in this town . . . all sorts of engraved and cut Drinking-Glasses, Dessert-Glasses . . . cut smelling bottles of all colours. To be sold . . . by Mrs. Annie Miles from the Hay Market, London." It may be assumed that many of the glass smelling bottles were blue, the most common color used for this purpose. In 1766 the German-born London glass cutter Christopher Haedy advertised in Bath " . . . great variety of Cut, Engraved and Gilt glasses including blue stands for Pickles. . . ."

It may reasonably be assumed that blue glass was being cut in the years just before the middle of the eighteenth century, and the Corning bowls illustrated here were probably made at the same time. In the Toledo Museum of Art there is a pair of covered blue glass cups, over a foot high, which are mounted in silver gilt by the London silversmith Thomas Heming, the mounts hallmarked for 1752–53. These cups stand on flattened knops above domed feet, much like the Corning bowls, and the cutting of these elements is closely similar, as is the scalloping of the feet. The two pairs must be very close in date.

English, probably London; mid-18th century.
Height: 14.5 cm (left); 14.2 cm (right).
Diameter (rim): 14.1 cm (both)

Cut-glass Fruit or Salad Bowl on a Pressed Foot

In 1746 an Act of Parliament in London imposed a tax on glass by weight and at the same time forbade the import of any foreign glass into Ireland or the export of any glass whatsoever from Ireland. The glass industry of Ireland had therefore no incentive to develop beyond what was adequate to furnish the home market, and in practice Dublin was the only effective center of glass manufacture until the American Revolution. This event stirred up a variety of existing resentments in Ireland, notable among them a desire for free trade, which was finally achieved in 1780 after determined agitation. Free trade without taxation, however, immediately gave the Irish glassmaker the advantage over his English competitor, and after 1780 the Irish industry mushroomed, usually staffed by immigrant English labor and partially financed by English capital. Apart from Dublin and Belfast (which opened its doors in 1776), new centers included Waterford and Cork, and many new glasshouses opened in all four centers between 1780 and 1825. In that year a tax comparable with that which had afflicted English glassmaking since 1746 was imposed on Irish glass, and the Irish industry began to decline.

Since much skilled labor in the Irish glass industry came from England, it was natural that the styles of manufacture and decoration in the two countries should be alike, and that it should in consequence be difficult to distinguish Irish products from English. All the cut elements decorating the bowl illustrated here were at home in England, and the pressed foot exemplifies a technique probably developed by the English "glass pinchers," craftsmen who flourished in Birmingham. Yet this boat-shaped vessel is one traditionally associated with Ireland, and is indeed probably Irish. Its cutting represents probably the high point of the technique in the British Isles, when the motifs were so chosen and attuned as to bring out to the full the light-refractive quality of the glass material, without in any way affecting the form to its detriment. The same tact is observable in the pressed foot, which—as is not always the case—produces a comparable play of light without being in any way disproportionate to the size of the bowl. One may imagine this bowl as the centerpiece in some such scene as that conjured up by the Duc de la Rochefoucauld, who visited England in 1784: ". . . the cloth is removed and you behold the most beautiful table that it is possible to see . . . their tables are made of most beautiful wood and always have a brilliant polish like that of the finest glass. After the removal of the cloth, the table is covered with all kinds of wine. . . . On the middle of the table there is a small quantity of fruit. . . . At this point all the servants disappear. The ladies drink a glass or two of wine and at the end of half an hour all go out together. It is then that real enjoyment begins. . . . One proceeds to drink—sometimes in an alarming measure. . . ."

Probably Irish,
Dublin or Cork;
c. 1790.
Diameter: 38.5 cm

77

Cut and Engraved Goblet with Silhouettes

The word "silhouette" is derived from the name of Étienne de Silhouette (1709–1767), a Controller General of Finances in France, whose favorite hobby was cutting profiles from black paper. Although the idea was not new, it was only after 1770 that it achieved general popularity. The art of making silhouettes was given added seriousness from 1775 onward (no. 79) by Johann Casper Lavater's *Essays on Physiognomy Calculated to Extend the Knowledge and Love of Mankind*. Lavater advanced the view that plain profiles in black were a true guide to character—the line of nose, forehead, and chin being more important diagnostically than other features. Accuracy in silhouettes was therefore of prime importance, and no less a person than Goethe helped Lavater to devise a chair designed to keep the head immobile while the silhouette was being drawn or cut. Most silhouettes were on paper or plaster, but a number were made in a variation of the *verre églomisé* technique, the black profile showing up on a gold ground, or sometimes the reverse. These were most frequently mounted and framed for hanging on the wall, but a more elaborate and expensive method involved the enclosure of these profiles in glass vessels.

Small medallions with gold motifs usually against a backing of red lacquer had been a frequent ornament of flasks and other types of vessels in Bohemia during the mid-eighteenth century, the medallions being inserted into cavities specially prepared for them in the surface of the glass. About 1780 this technique, requiring the collaboration of a skilled glass cutter, was applied to the silhouette portrait. The main center for this work appears to have been Warmbrunn in Silesia. Many surviving examples—usually vases with cut feet and cutting around the base—have portraits of the Prussian royal family, Silesia being by this date a part of Prussia. At least one glass is known with a wheel-engraved view of the Riesengebirge range supplementing the gold silhouettes, which argues for an origin in Warmbrunn (no. 67).

A number of glasses with this type of decoration are signed by Johann Sigismund Menzel (1744–1810) of Warmbrunn, and others of the same sort may reasonably be attributed to him. Two of these signed portraits bear the date 1789. Apart from the cutting, these glasses are often wheel engraved with frame settings for portraits and with a pearl border below the rim. The Corning beaker (which lacks its cover) no doubt represents a husband and wife with their child in a smaller medallion below. An almost identical glass is in the Metropolitan Museum, New York.

Silesian, Warmbrunn;
c. 1790.
Height: 17.8 cm

78

Beaker Painted in Transparent Enamels

A curious phenomenon in the history of the arts is an idea that can be "in the air" at a given moment, yet gone the next. In Germany painting in transparent enamels on vessel glass and the art of stained glass flourished together in the seventeenth century (no. 49), and both languished in the following century. At the beginning of the nineteenth century the revival of stained glass was again almost exactly contemporaneous with the revivification of painting in transparent enamels on vessels. Yet this development did not take place in a vacuum. In England the art of stained glass had been kept precariously alive throughout the eighteenth century, notably by William Peckitt toward the end, and thereafter by such artists as James and Eglington Margaret Pearson, and W. R. Eginton, all of whom survived into the early years of the nineteenth century, when the taste for gothic church art was on the increase. This was also a period when colored "transparencies" were popular at times of public celebration.

The leading figure in the stained glass revival in Germany was Michael Sigismund Frank, whose first windows were produced in 1804. A glass tumbler enameled in transparent enamels is inscribed, "For M. S. Frank in Nuremberg from S. Mohn in Leipzig 1808." It also bears the silhouette self-portrait of the artist, Samuel Mohn. Later, Mohn's son, Gottlob Samuel Mohn (1789–1825), was also in contact with Frank and in 1823 offered to buy his enamel recipes, which revealed that his own most successful formula was one "which I had from England."

Samuel Mohn (1762–1815) was not a man of artistic training, and at the time of his son's birth he appears to have been a soldier. He was an enterprising and technical-minded person who was particularly interested in making colored enamels. He could also paint silhouettes and simple decorative motifs, starting his career as a decorator of porcelain cups and saucers, the earliest known dating from 1803. At this date he was in Halle, but in the difficult years of the Napoleonic Wars he led a peripatetic life, traveling with his family to Berlin, Fürsten Isenburg, Leipzig, Stettin, Neubrandenburg, then Berlin again, and finally, at the end of 1806, back to Leipzig. Here Samuel Mohn finally set up "a small workshop" in which he produced "drinking glasses of all sorts with landscapes, allegories, ornaments, and music with words." Here, too, Gottlob had the opportunity of studying drawing under J. V. Schnorr von Carolsfeld; later, when the family moved to Dresden in 1808, he studied under a drawing master named Lindner. He was therefore academically a better-trained artist than his father, and he rivaled him even in his own chosen field of the silhouette.

In the Dresden workshop Samuel Mohn employed not only his son (until he left for Vienna in 1811), but also a number of other assistants, and it is in many instances impossible to say who in the Mohn workshop painted a particular piece. In 1811 Mohn published in a Dresden newspaper a tariff of his productions. Various views in and around Dresden were among the cheapest items, including "Meissen" (shown here) costing eight Thaler. The advertisement continued, "A flower border raises the price by two to four Thaler." The vine border on the Corning beaker is an unusual variant, the more normal being of laurel or oak leaves, roses, or pansies. The beaker is signed "S. Mohn fec."

German, Dresden;
c. 1810.
Height: 10.2 cm

Meissen

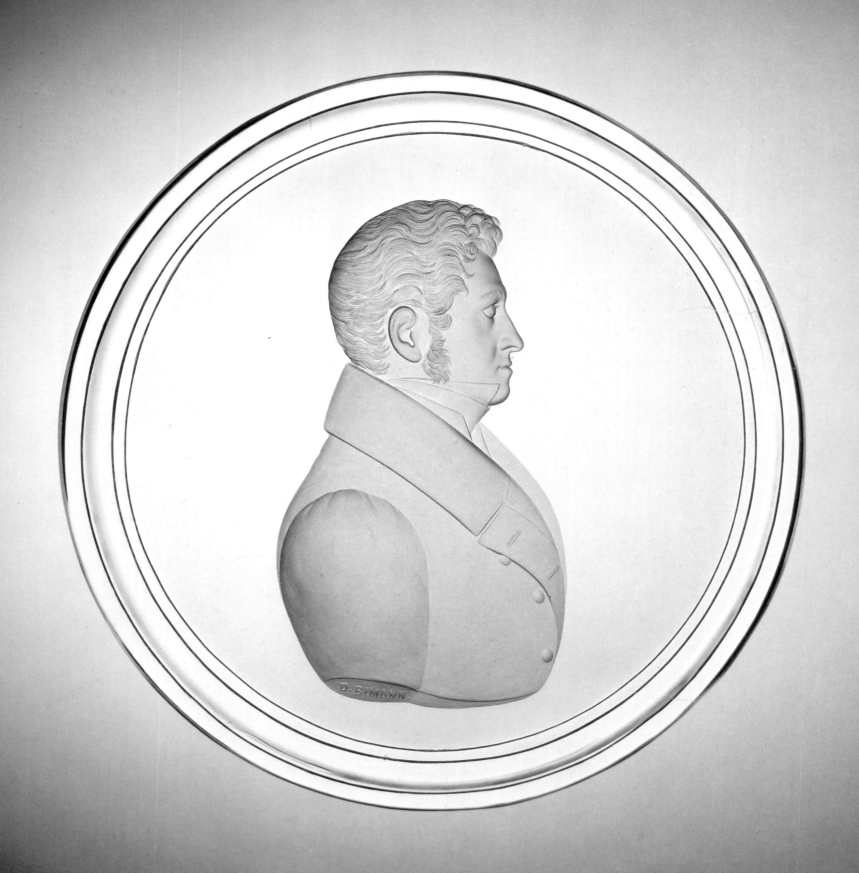

79

Wheel-engraved Portrait Medallion

Dominik Biemann was born April 1, 1800, as the fourth child of an employee of the Harrachov glassworks, not far from Liberec, in the north of modern Czechoslovakia. The family was poor, but his godfather was Johann Pohl, manager of the glassworks, and at the age of seven Dominik started work there as a carrier. In due course he was apprenticed to Franz Pohl, elder brother of Johann Pohl and a first-rate wheel engraver. At the age of twenty-six he migrated to Prague, where his brother Franz was studying medicine, and the following year he was admitted as a citizen and thereby acquired the right to carry on his trade of engraver. In 1826 he enrolled in the School (later the Academy) of Art in Prague, where he probably learned to draw and became familiar with some of the classical subjects that he later engraved on his glasses. At the Academy's exhibition of 1829 he exhibited seven engravings, including two portraits, a copy of Raphael's *Madonna della Sedia*, a *Descent from the Cross*, and two riding and hunting subjects of the sort popular at the time. Later in the same year he entered these and other pieces in the Bohemian Industrial Exhibition in Prague and received a silver medal. From 1826 onward he worked in the summer season at Franzensbad, a spa resort frequented by the nobility and the richer bourgeoisie, who at this time of rapidly increasing prosperity were exerting an ever greater influence on contemporary life. It was now that Biemann acquired a special reputation for portraiture, and this side of his work remained of dominant importance to him, both economically and psychologically, until—toward the middle of the century—mechanically produced forms of portraiture, such as the daguerreotype, began to eat into the market for wheel-engraved portraits. At the same time he was engraving portraits for personal customers in Franzensbad, he was producing glasses engraved with popular subjects, including hunting and coaching scenes, for commercial dealers such as the Steigerwald firm of Frankfurt and Würzburg.

Portrait engraving was Biemann's forte, and this predilection was probably intimately connected with his neurotic temperament. Apparently for economic reasons he set his face against marrying the woman he loved in favor of a rich wife who never materialized, and he became increasingly obsessed with money and worried by fears of poverty until in 1855 he was driven to attempt suicide. He was something of a religious maniac, obsessed with the Madonna. He wrote in his diary in 1837: "I dreamed I saw the Madonna floating high up in the lustre of the stars. . . . This dream came to me repeatedly." His overwrought state of mind perhaps led to his repeated use of the Madonna theme and the idealization of the grace of young women observable in his portrait medallions. He was also, however, a serious student of the contemporary theories of physiognomy, and in 1841 he compiled a manuscript, "Observations on the Physiognomy of the Facial Features," illustrating it by his own ink sketches. This intensely serious concern with likeness and character comes out in his wheel-engraved portrait medallions, particularly those of men. Like Christian Gottfried Schneider of Warmbrunn before him (no. 67), he seems to have drawn better with the wheel than with the pen.

Bohemian, probably Franzensbad; dated 1834.
Diameter: 9.5 cm

175

80

Goblet with Cut, Engraved, Stained, and Enameled Decoration

Bohemia had been the training ground of wheel engravers ever since the seventeenth century, and in the third quarter of the nineteenth century it produced some of the greatest artists ever to practice the technique (no. 91). Developments in Bohemia in this period, however, tended to veer away from the pure form of this art on crystal glass to an ever increasing use of color, a concept that progressively pushed into the background the idea of glass as crystal, to be decorated only by wheel cutting and engraving. This seesaw of taste may be traced in many epochs of glass history.

Toward the middle of the nineteenth century the Bohemian trade was determined to gild the lily in a way previously unparalleled, with a lack of restraint that matched the economic ebullience and self-confidence of the rising mercantile middle class. In this "Biedermeier" period, more of anything could only be good. The goblet here illustrates this principle in essence. Its elaborate profile has been carved out in depth (note the "jewels" on the uppermost knop) and then cut into broad vertical facets overall. The foot has been deeply notched to produce a hexafoil plan, the individual "leaves" of which have been elaborately cut into "hobnail" diamonds on the underside. Parts of the goblet have been overlaid with a yellow surface stain, which on the underside of the foot has been cut into a sixteen-point star. This in turn is surrounded by a wreath of flowers painted in translucent enamels on a black ground that has been etched with a *vermiculée* design showing the transparent yellow stain through the black. Translucent enamels are also used for rendering the coats-of-arms that decorate the back and sides of the goblet. In the front is a wheel-engraved view (cut through yellow stain) of the dedication on September 29, 1835, of the monument commemorating the battle of Kulm (northern Bohemia) in 1813. Only gilding is needed to complete the total repertoire of the decorating shop, and this is not infrequently found on other cut, engraved, and enameled pieces, especially those made for the oriental market.

Three virtually identical glasses must have been made to this pattern, of which one was preserved in the Hohenzollern Museum, Berlin, the second in the Technical Museum, Vienna; it is evident that these glasses were commissioned for presentation to representatives of the allied forces gathered to oppose Napoleon at the battle of Kulm. The arms of Austria, Prussia, and Russia are painted on the glasses. The goblets originally had covers in the form of an elaborate openwork crown surmounted with a cross and orb and supported on a cushion with tassels at the corners. Not surprisingly, these elaborate confections have been broken in succeeding years. It is believed that these glasses were made at Neuwelt, in northern Bohemia.

Bohemian,
probably 1835.
Height: 25.6 cm

Table of Colored Cut Glass Mounted in Ormolu

In December 1756, Lady Mary Wortley Montagu, the famous English bluestocking, wrote from Padua to her daughter in England concerning her experiences in Venice, "I was showed (of their own invention) a set of furniture, in a taste entirely new; it consists of eight large armed-chairs, the same number of sconces, a table, and prodigious looking-glass, all of glass. It is impossible to imagine their beauty; they deserve being placed in a prince's dressing-room, or grand cabinet; the price demanded is £400." A single armchair of extravagant baroque design survives at Murano to illustrate Lady Mary's observations. It is mainly of carved wood, with inlays of royal blue glass.

The fashion for glass-covered furniture was by no means restricted to Venice. In the third quarter of the eighteenth century a factory at Brunswick produced long-case clocks, cabinets, and other types of furniture covered with mirror plate elaborately wheel engraved. This extreme taste, which might be compared with the vogue for silver furniture in the seventeenth century, found an enthusiastic response in Imperial Russia. As early as the 1760s a set of console tables was made for the Chinese Palace in Oranienbaum (near St. Petersburg), the tops formed of a mosaic of colored opaque glasses from the great scientist M. V. Lomonosov's glasshouse at Ust-Ruditskaia. The tables were made up at the Peterhof lapidary factory with lavish excrescences of fruit decorating the wooden frames. Lomonosov's preoccupation with colored glasses carried over after his death into the general glass production of late eighteenth-century Russia. Added to the blue, purple, emerald green, and opaque white that were more or less the common property of European glassmaking at this period were a number of intermediate colors. The taste for glass encrustations also persisted. An ebony bureau surviving at Pavlovsk is decorated all over with *verre églomisé* plaques bearing the portraits of the Emperor Paul I (reigned 1796–1801), his consort, and their daughters. During the reign of his mother, Catherine II, glass was extensively used to decorate her palace at Pushkin. The architect was a Scot named Charles Cameron, who must have been aware of the use of glass for interior decoration by his countryman John Adam (notably the glass drawing room made for the duke of Northumberland's London house in 1773–75). At Pushkin, Cameron created a room in which the walls were covered by blue-and-white glass plaques with gilt bronze motifs mounted on blue roundels, while blue glass columns framed the doors, mounted on an underlay of silver filigree. The room has unfortunately been destroyed, but a card table decorated *en suite* with it survives, the legs of blue transparent glass, and the top formed of squares of blue over silver filigree, with white squares in the corners.

All these decorations were made essentially by inlaying and encrusting with glass armatures made of different materials. It remained for the nineteenth century to make the furniture itself virtually entirely of large pieces of glass. The table illustrated here was made of a single slab of blue glass cut to an octagon and resting on a columnar support made of a single piece of amber-colored glass decorated with spiral cutting. This in turn rests on a square plinth of amber glass so dark that it appears black. All these components are held together and embellished by elements of gilt bronze. The whole was designed by A. N. Voronikhin in 1804 and was made up at the Imperial factory. With it originally went a ewer and basin of blue and crystal glass, wheel cut with relief diamonds and mounted in ormolu of the highest quality.

Russian, St. Petersburg; c. 1804.
Height: 79 cm

Red Overlay Vase with Wheel-engraved Decoration

Glassmaking has always sat somewhat uneasily in the company of the other Chinese arts. There is little continuity observable in its development, from the characteristic asymmetrical "eye beads" of the Chou period (c. 1122–256 B.C.), through the small molded objects imitating ritual jades in the Han dynasty (202 B.C.–A.D. 221), to the scattered vessels of uncertain date that have come to light in China in the last hundred years. It is admitted by Chinese historical sources that the main inspiration for Chinese glassmaking, and not infrequently the glassmakers themselves, came from the West.

It was only with the end of the Ming dynasty (1368–1644) that evidence gradually became available from non-Chinese sources. Father Matteo Ricci (d. 1610), who was largely responsible for the success of the Jesuit mission in China from 1583 onward, and who astonished the Chinese court by demonstrating prisms of Venetian glass, recorded his observation that "at the present time they make glass, but inferior enough to our own." Unfortunately, this says nothing of the Chinese methods of manufacture. It seems likely, however, that the Jesuit mission was instrumental in introducing glassblowing into the glass workshops that the Emperor K'ang Hsi (1662–1722) set up within the Forbidden City in Peking. The success of this venture may be judged from the fact that in 1721 the emperor sent as part of a diplomatic gift to Pope Clement XI no fewer than 136 vases of "Peking glass," although they were lost on the voyage to Europe. A series of blown vessels has been attributed to this phase of Chinese glassmaking; usually of a grayish-colorless "crystal," but often also of blue glass, they were frequently rib molded and usually characterized by the defect of crizzling so often found also in contemporary European glass (no. 56). Some of the later examples bear the mark of the Emperor Yung Chêng, and it was in his reign (1722–36), and more particularly in that of his successor, Ch'ien Lung, that the character of Chinese glass was formed. This shows a reversion to the older tradition of copying vessels normally made by carving from a solid block of natural stone. Glassblowing still continued, but mainly in the subordinate role of providing blanks for embellishment by the lapidary.

Among the great technical innovations in the Chinese porcelain industry in the early eighteenth century had been the production of opaque enamels, and particularly the rose pink which gave the *famille rose* its name. Its technical roots were in the European glass industry, where the "purple of Cassius," produced by precipitating gold with tin, had been used to make ruby glass since before 1679. In China this ruby glass was the most widely used casing material on vessels destined to be cut in the cameo technique. Snuff bottles of this sort are among the most common Chinese glasses of the eighteenth and nineteenth centuries.

The bottle shown here is of uncommon size and has been skillfully wheel cut through the ruby layer down to the characteristically flocculent colorless glass below with its frosted appearance. The ruby layer itself has been subtly worked into a three-dimensional perspective of considerable depth. The scene represents four galloping horsemen brandishing racket-shaped objects in both hands, a fifth holding a pair of lances. On the neck is a temple building with four men on a veranda, apparently inspecting a votive tablet. All these figures are shown in a landscape of craggy rocks with cloud scrolls wreathing their tops and with trees of various species clearly differentiated.

Chinese,
probably reign of
Emperor Ch'ien Lung (1736–96).
Height: 48.9 cm.
Gift of Benjamin D. Bernstein

Handled Jar
with Wheel-engraved
and Gilt Decoration

No doubt motivated by the demand for window glass created by the royal palaces, a Catalán glassman named Ventura Sit in 1728 left the Nuevo Baztán glasshouse, to the southeast of Madrid, and moved to San Ildefonso, near the palace of La Granja. Here he built a glasshouse that in due course came under royal patronage and went on to become the best-known factory in Europe for the making of plate glass, being capable of producing the largest mirrors known at that time, big enough to reflect the image of a rider on horseback. For mirrors, the best possible crystal glass was needed, and the factory management was at pains to improve the quality of its material, even going to the lengths of commissioning a translation into Spanish of Antonio Neri's *L'arte Vetraria*, the standard textbook of glass technology at that date.

Ventura Sit directed the factory until his death in 1755, but before that date a separate workshop had been set up to make blown tablewares decorated by cutting and engraving. The making of plate glass for mirrors had long been a French specialty, and the arts of wheel cutting and engraving had their roots, and found their best practitioners, in Germany and Bohemia. It was not unnatural, therefore, that a number of French, German, and even Swedish craftsmen migrated to San Ildefonso to practice their skills. The glass made at San Ildefonso, therefore, has something of an international character. Yet the shapes of the glass are characteristically Spanish, and the wheel engraving, although essentially like that ornamenting the Bohemian glasses imported in bulk at this time into Spain, has an entirely individual character. Surviving signed panels, furthermore, show that the foreign masters had exceptionally able Spanish pupils such as Felix Ramos and Antonio Juan.

A common feature of engraved La Granja glasses is that the engraving has been gilt, a practice not unknown in Germany and elsewhere but more general at San Ildefonso. The factory's process of fire gilding has been laid to the credit of Sigismund Brun, a German from Hanover who was in charge of one of the workshops making blown tablewares. Gilt decoration painted directly onto the glass is also known from the factory, and the gilding has proved its durability in use.

The style of the San Ildefonso factory was dictated by the growing eighteenth-century vogue for engraved glasses "in the Bohemian manner," but in the case of the Corning jar illustrated, the masters have reverted to an earlier manner in crowning the cover with a pincered finial recalling the elaborate furnace work of the *façon de Venise*. This is repeated inside the vessel, on the base, a further reminiscence of Venetian glassmaking in which such tricks were common.

Spanish, La Granja de San Ildefonso; c. 1775. Height (with cover): 32.5 cm

Wheel-engraved Tumbler and Cover

The three leading entrepreneurs in the development of glassmaking in the eighteenth-century United States were all of German origin—Caspar Wistar (no. 85), "Baron" Henry William Stiegel, who built three glasshouses in Pennsylvania between 1763 and 1774, and Johann Friedrich Amelung. Amelung (b. 1741) came from near Hanover, and started his career as a farm manager. In 1773, however, his elder brother leased the duke of Brunswick's mirror factory at Grünenplan, south of Hanover, and Johann Friedrich joined him as manager. Mirrors were both blown and cast at Grünenplan, and Amelung must have acquired a thorough knowledge of the glass industry. The financial position of the Grünenplan factory deteriorated steadily in the decade 1773–83, and he decided to migrate to America to found a glass factory there. A meeting in Bremen with a Baltimore merchant named Benjamin Crockett induced Amelung to decide on Maryland for his venture, and Bremen merchants offered him financial support. He gathered together glassworkers from Bohemia and Germany, and with a capital of ten thousand pounds, the equipment for three furnaces, and sixty men, he set sail in the spring of 1784, arriving in Baltimore on August 31. He had introductions from some of the most influential Americans then in Europe, including Benjamin Franklin and John Adams, to some of the leading political and commercial figures in the U.S.A., including General Thomas Mifflin, to whom in 1791 Amelung dedicated a handsome engraved goblet. In December 1784, Amelung purchased an existing glassworks, which had been set up by six Germans from Stiegel's Mannheim works, on its closure in 1774. This factory was in Frederick County, some forty miles to the west of Baltimore, and with it Amelung acquired some two thousand acres of land, partly wooded for the provision of fuel and potash. As early as February 1785, he advertised in the *Maryland Journal and Baltimore Adviser* his intention to make "all kinds of glass-Wares, viz. Window-Glass, from the lowest to the finest sorts, white and green Bottles, Wines and other Drinking-Glasses, as also Optical Glasses, and Looking-Glasses, finished compleat." Finds on the factory site indicate that Amelung in fact made glasses of the types indicated, as well as others not mentioned. Ironically, he was never to make mirrors, for which his training would ideally have qualified him.

In August 1785, Amelung renamed his estate "New Bremen" as a tribute to his German backers. This name gave the clue to the identification of Amelung's most ambitious work when, in 1928, a covered goblet was found in Bremen inscribed, "Old Bremen Success and the New Progress" and "New Bremen Glassmanufactory. 1788 North America State of Maryland." Since then a number of Amelung glasses have been identified. They are of high quality both in material and glassmanship, the latter evidently inspired by the English-style glasses made at Lauenstein, near Hanover. The engraver, clearly a German, as his misspellings occasionally reveal, although technically not up to the highest German standard, has a style of his own that is full of charm. He was clearly schooled in the rococo period, and his stock of motifs was outmoded by the 1780s. He nevertheless managed to combine them with inscriptions in an open, fresh style that had much of the neoclassical feeling about it. The Corning covered beaker illustrated is inscribed "Happy is he who is blessed with virtuous Children. Carolina Lucia Amelung. 1788" and was made for Amelung's wife. It shows Tobias (the model of a virtuous child) and the Angel following a little dog over a patch of land ingenuously bounded by rococo scrollwork and flowers.

American,
New Bremen, Maryland;
dated 1788.
Height: 30.1 cm

Covered Sugar Bowl of Blown and Tooled Glass

American,
Southern New Jersey;
c. 1750–77.
Height: 15.5 cm

It is a curious fact that glassmaking, one of the most sophisticated forms of industrial art, should have been among the first to be started in the New World. In 1608 the Virginia Company sent from England to Jamestown, Virginia, aboard the *Mary and Margaret*, "eight Dutchmen and Poles" (probably Germans, some perhaps from Silesia) who were to make pitch, potash, and glass, all products of the forests that were known to abound in the New World and that were in shrinking supply in England. Some glass was made and samples were sent back to England. The only remaining glass from this venture is in the form of tiny fragments of green vials and window glass found on the glasshouse site. The attempt foundered, perhaps as a result of famine in the winter of 1609–10, and when a second attempt was made in 1621, the aim had changed. Instead of glassmen brought up in the "forest" tradition of Germany, the company sent out Italian glassworkers mainly to make beads for the Indian trade. Not surprisingly, this was a total failure, since the Italians were not able to use the skills from their native tradition.

Once the infant colonies on the eastern seaboard were established and growing, the situation changed entirely. Now their needs had to be met, and these were preeminently for window glass and bottles. The colonies were regarded by the English government as a market for English-made goods, and in fact window glass and bottles were supplied in enormous quantities from England, especially from the glassmaking and mercantile city of Bristol. A few sporadic efforts were made in the seventeenth century to start an indigenous production (Salem, Massachusetts, New York, and Philadelphia), and the amount of glass increased in the eighteenth century. However, it was government policy to discourage such enterprises. In consequence, information about them is unreliable as well as scarce. Best documented is the enterprise of one Caspar Wistar, who in 1717 emigrated from Germany to Pennsylvania, where he first learned the art of button making and then set up a store in Philadelphia. Here he became a prominent member of the Quaker community, and in due course he acquired two thousand acres of woodland in Salem County, southern New Jersey.

In 1738 four German glassblowers arrived in Philadelphia to take up partnership with Wistar on terms that gave them a third of the proceeds of the joint enterprise. A glasshouse was built at Alloways Creek and production started before the end of 1739. The "Wistarburgh" works produced bottles in great quantity (of which one surviving example has been identified) and window glass, described slightingly by Governor William Franklin as "very coarse Green Glass for Windows, used only in some of the Houses of the poorer Sort of People." The glasshouse, however, also produced green and colorless table glass; candlesticks, baskets, and a small group of handled bowls with covers have been identified as Wistarburgh products. The bowl illustrated here, which came from a family home at Glassboro, New Jersey, fits well into the category of covered bowls made by the Wistar concern, although it is also possible that it was made somewhat later at one of a number of other glassworks which opened in southern New Jersey. The aesthetic appeal of this glass, with its simple form and decoration and beautiful green material, is fully equal to that of the glasses made in Renaissance Germany in the *Waldglas* tradition, one to which these early American glasses strictly belong.

Sugar Bowl of Amber Glass with Mold-blown Ribbing

As the settlers of the post-Revolutionary years in America steadily moved westward and their numbers swelled, the demand for glass also increased in direct ratio with the difficulty of transporting such a fragile commodity over long distances. There was also a natural tendency for glassmakers themselves to migrate to western territories, where the clearance of virgin forest was an essential precondition of agriculture and where timber for fuel was in consequence very cheap. Probably the most important early move westward beyond the Appalachians was the 1797 founding of a bottle-making factory at Pittsburgh, Pennsylvania. Pittsburgh, at the junction of the Allegheny and Ohio rivers, was exceptionally well placed to send its products northward on the former and toward the southwest and the basin of the Mississippi on the latter.

In 1825 the Erie Canal, linking Albany with Buffalo, facilitated the trade from eastern New York State toward Ohio, and in 1834 the Main Line Canal was built to connect Pittsburgh and Philadelphia. In consequence, there was a far freer movement of commerce in both directions, for many of the farmers in the newly opened areas paid for what they needed in kind and not in cash. Window glass and bottles, as hitherto, were the glass commodities most in demand, but they were difficult to transport without heavy loss, although water transport greatly improved the chances of safe arrival. Vessel glass was far less in demand, and a traveler in the early nineteenth century could comment, "For want of a glass . . . from which to drink, if you are offered whisky (which is the principal drink here) the bottle is presented to you or a bowl or a teacup containing the liquor."

Pittsburgh became a great glassmaking center and remained so until the end of the nineteenth century; it was via Pittsburgh that many glassmakers went into the new territories of western Virginia, Kentucky, and especially Ohio. Here some eight glasshouses, some of only short duration, were founded before 1825. Of these one of the most important was the White Glass Works at Zanesville on the Muskingum River, where the covered sugar bowl shown here was most probably made.

Since Pittsburgh was the main center of diffusion in the Midwest, it was natural enough that many of the characteristics of Pittsburgh vessel glass should also be found again in Ohio. These tablewares—milk bowls, jugs, salts, bottles, and other simple shapes—were normally a sideline of glasshouses that otherwise specialized in window- or bottle-glass production, and they tended therefore to be made of the material currently in use—sometimes an aquamarine green if made in a window house, brown or blue if made in a bottle house. At Pittsburgh much use was made of simple molds that broke up the surface of the glass to give glancing optical effects. These were mainly plain rib molds giving vertical ribs that could, if wished, be twisted or "swirled"; for further elaboration the swirled ribbing could be blown again into the mold to produce "broken swirl" patterns. The Zanesville bowl here has been blown into a twenty-four-ribbed mold, characteristic of this factory, and the glassmaker has had the tact to leave the ribbing vertical so that it picks up the ribs on the double-domed cover. This cover and the wide-shouldered form tend to distinguish the Ohio glass from that made farther east. The handsome color and the glorious shape, with the line of the body running unbroken into the line of the cover, make this a glass to rank with the greatest masterpieces of earlier glassblowing.

American, probably Zanesville, Ohio; c. 1815–30. Diameter: 13 cm

87

Jug and Covered Sugar Bowl with Furnace-worked Decoration

American, New York;
c. 1835–50.
Diameter (rim): 10.9 cm.
Height: 16.4 cm

Somewhat the same economic conditions as had affected Pennsylvania and Ohio (no. 86) also worked on the glass industry in New York State, where the main emphasis was again on bottles and window glass. The window houses no doubt produced the aquamarine glasses characteristic of New York State, as exemplified in the pieces illustrated here.

Glasses of this character were not a normal part of current production, but were made by the glassblowers in their spare time, usually as gifts to friends or relatives or as commissions for others with a similar intent. The glassworkers of New York State brought with them, or learned locally, many of the tricks of glass decoration characteristic of New Jersey glasshouses. These included threading, as seen around the neck of the jug opposite, pincered work such as was responsible for the modeling of the hen surmounting the bowl, and above all, "lily pad" decoration, a technique that reached its highest fulfillment and widest distribution in the United States. It consisted of taking an additional gather at the base of the parison, and then drawing this extra glass up into tapering projections which terminate in a rounded lobe formed by the surplus glass accumulating around the tool. These were sometimes flattened, and the arms themselves given a diagonal swirl. The aesthetic effect created by this technique may justly be compared with that of the applied decoration on the Frankish claw beakers of the sixth century (no. 22), although here the applied elements are hollow blown and connect with the interior of the vessel.

The Corning glasses are distinguished by the fact that, beyond the embellishments already described, they are made with hollow bulbs in the stems and below the finial of the bowl. These bulbs enclose silver half-dimes, those in the stems dated 1829 and that in the cover dated 1835, thus providing the earliest possible date for the making of the bowl. The two pieces came together from a New York State family, and are of a kind associated with glasshouses at Redwood (near Watertown) or Redford (near Plattsburgh), New York.

88

Early Mold-blown Pint Flask

One of the problems of making commercial containers in the eighteenth century had been that of maintaining a standard capacity in a free-blown article. Although the workmen attained incredible accuracy in making a parison of the right size and shaping it to a standard form, some variation was inevitable. In making ordinary wine and beer bottles it was not until 1821 that the Bristol firm of Ricketts produced a type of mold guaranteed to turn out an absolutely standard quart bottle. Well before that, however, small vials for patent medicines such as proliferated in the eighteenth century—Turlington's Balsam, Daffy's Elixir, Dalby's Carminative, and many more—had been made in two-piece molds that repeated these legends on each container turned out, as authentication of the contents rather than as a guarantee of capacity. It required no great stretch of imagination to combine these two principles in order to make containers that were both decorative and of standard capacity. This happened in America in the early decades of the nineteenth century, when whiskey as a commodity appears to have enjoyed an unparalleled popularity and diffusion.

The technique of mold blowing, probably as old as glassblowing itself, enabled designs of all kinds to be used to embellish the objects blown, and in due course all kinds of pictorial flasks were made to commemorate the events and personalities of contemporary American history. The earliest notice of such flasks dates from 1822, when "American Eagle, ship Franklin, Agricultural and Masonic Pocket Bottles" were advertised in Philadelphia. The type had certainly been in production before this, however, and the flask shown belongs to one of the earliest and rarest categories of these containers. On the reverse it bears the legend "JARED SPENCER" in a circle corresponding to the concentric circles on the side illustrated. A second variant of the same basic design bears the inscription "MANCHESTER.CON" in place of the purely formal design of the Corning flask, and there can be little doubt that both were made at the glasshouse started by William and Elisha Pitkin in 1783 at Manchester, near Hartford, Connecticut. Closely similar flasks bear the initials "J.P.F.," said to stand for J. P. Foster, who appears to have taken over the managership of the Pitkin Works in 1810. Since the Pitkin factory closed about 1830, the date of these flasks can be fairly closely established. The name "Jared Spencer" has never been explained.

The early mold-blown flasks of Syria are universally admired (no. 13) for their color and design, and rightly so. The same criteria should be applied to those of nineteenth-century America, and very often the latter show up triumphantly well. It should not be forgotten, however, that much of the credit must go to the mold-maker, of whom often very little is known. In some of the larger works, such as the Philadelphia glasshouse that issued the advertisement cited above, the moldmaker was a part of the regular staff. Smaller glasshouses, however, probably had to be content with commissions to outside moldmakers and to resign themselves to a certain similarity with the products of other factories. Such considerations probably did not weigh very heavily on proprietors engaged in the day-to-day struggles of commercial glass manufacture.

*American, probably
Manchester, Connecticut;
c. 1820.
Height: 17.8 cm*

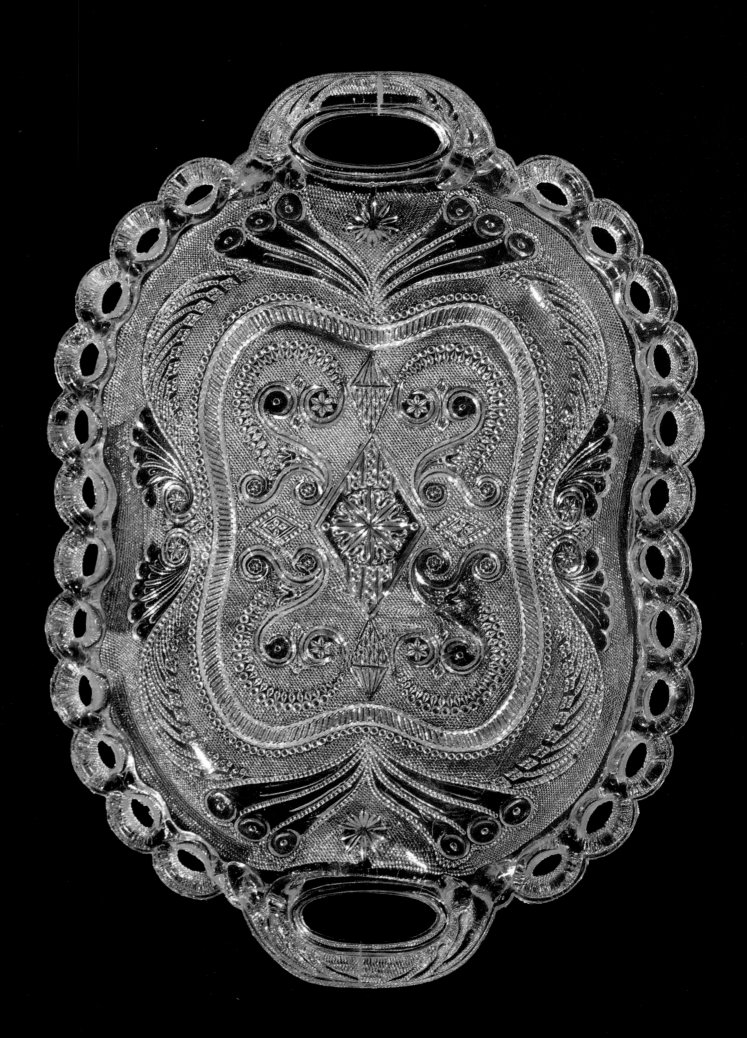

Pressed Glass Cake Plate

James Boardman, an Englishman visiting the U.S.A. in 1829, attended the fair of the American Institute of the City of New York in October of that year: "The most novel article was the pressed glass, which was far superior, both in design and execution, to anything of the kind I have ever seen either in London or elsewhere. The merit of the invention is due to the Americans, and it is likely to prove one of great national importance." It is unknown how deep Mr. Boardman's understanding of the glass industry was, but his testimony was confirmed by someone with genuine firsthand knowledge.

In 1849 Apsley Pellatt, perhaps the leading glassmaker of his day in London, wrote in his *Curiosities of Glass Making*, "The invention of pressing Glass by machinery has been introduced into England from the United States of America. . . ." It is probable, however, that the emphasis here should fall on the words "by machinery," for such things as the feet of bowls (no. 76) and saltcellars had been made by pressing since the end of the eighteenth century in Ireland and certainly also in England. This fact was pointed out by no less a person than Deming Jarves, himself not only the leading figure in the Boston and Sandwich Glass Company, but a prime mover in the development of pressing. In Ireland, indeed, molded dishes that appear to be pressed were made by, or on behalf of, two Dublin companies, of which one appears to have been dissolved as early as 1802. It is noteworthy that in his book Pellatt represented the process by a woodcut of two men working a simple press with a hand-operated lever, although earlier, in 1831, he himself had applied for a patent for a method of assembling molds and had included a detailed drawing of the far more complicated "machine for pressing glass by the mode lately introduced from America." The first American patents themselves, beginning in 1825, were for small objects such as doorknobs, which could be made by the simple tools of the "glass-pincher." By 1827, however, Deming Jarves was already pressing small cup plates and saltcellars, and perhaps had succeeded in producing tumblers with imitated cut-glass designs. From 1828 onward Jarves and a number of other manufacturers brought out a whole series of patents for the improvement of the machinery used in pressing.

At first there was a natural tendency for makers to copy in pressed glass the complicated designs of the far more expensive cut-glass, but the technique had its disadvantages. As Pellatt wrote in 1849, ". . . by the contact of the metal plunger with the Glass, the latter loses much of the brilliant transparency so admired in cut Glass." In addition, the glass material itself was often flawed or bubbled, and these defects showed up badly in the finished object. Other types of design were therefore developed that concealed these blemishes and the surface-dimming imparted by the chilling contact of the metal mold. This was achieved by using overall stippling as a background to the larger elements in the design. The glass of this character is usually referred to as "lacy." The cake plate shown here is one of the most ambitious and successful of these designs, not least in its use of an openwork rim border. The tray was almost certainly made at the Boston and Sandwich Glass Company directed by Deming Jarves himself. As early as 1831–32 the firm was listed in a directory as making "Plain and Cut, Flint and Enameled Glass and Pressed Ware."

American, probably Sandwich, Massachusetts; c. 1830–40.
Length: 30 cm

Paperweight Enclosing the Figure of a Salamander

The glass paperweight came into the marketplace, it appears, in 1845. Its origins are uncertain, since both Venetian and French examples bear the date 1845. The general opinion in the past has been that the idea was introduced into France by Eugène Péligot, a professor at the Conservatoire des Arts et Métiers in Paris and later the author of a book on glassmaking. In 1845 Péligot visited the Exhibition of Austrian Industry in Vienna and saw there the paperweights made by the Venetian manufacturer Pietro Bigaglia, Venice being at this date a dependency of the Austrian Empire. It seems unlikely, however, that the French paperweights that appeared in the same year could have been copied and perfected in such a short space of time. Moreover, the French excelled the Venetians in their paperweights by the perfection of their technique and in particular by their use of a high dome of pure crystal glass to magnify the tiny motifs used to decorate the weight. These motifs were normally flowers made by the millefiori technique and comparable canes with formal designs, either laid pell-mell or arranged concentrically or in loops and swirls. The classic period for the French paperweight, between 1845 and 1855, was dominated by three glasshouses—Clichy, Baccarat, and Saint-Louis.

By the middle of the nineteenth century another technique had been added to the millefiori method. Motifs, mainly flowers and fruits, but occasionally animals, birds, and reptiles, were made by lampworking and were then covered by the crystal dome. The lampworker, whose craft can be traced to the fifth century B.C., sat at a table and created small figures or scientific equipment as need dictated, using rods and tubes of glass melted in the flame of a lamp. The lamp was set on the table in front of him and controlled by a foot-operated bellows.

There appears to have been a revival of paperweight manufacture in the 1870s, and a number of weights which do not appear to fit into the *oeuvre* of the "classic" factories mentioned above may have been made elsewhere at this later date. The U.S. Commissioners to the Paris Exposition of 1878 indeed described "Paperweights of solid glass, containing glass snakes, lizards, squirrels, and flowers . . . a coiled snake, with head erect, of two colored glasses cut in spots to show both colors. . . ." These were exhibited by the Pantin factory of Monot Père et fils et Stumpf, Pantin being a suburb of Paris. The Corning weight shown here is decorated with a small lizard whose body is made of a cased glass that has been cut on the wheel to simulate the creature's scales, before the legs and other accessories were added at the lamp. This seems to agree with the description of the Pantin lizard and supports the attribution of the weight to this factory. At a later date (1880) the firm gave a "*presse-papier, fleurs et salamandre*" ("paperweight, flowers, and salamander") to the Paris Conservatoire des Arts et Métiers.

The Corning weight is noteworthy for its technical competence. The difficulty of overlaying the three-dimensional figure with crystal in such a way that bubbles were not trapped has been completely overcome. The covering dome is of flawless crystal, and the ground on which the lizard stands is cleverly made of fragments of green glass and what appears to be ground-up refractory material from the melting pots. When they were made, paperweights like these could have been bought quite cheaply in the shops of stationers and others selling fancy goods. In 1849 a Baccarat snake weight, the most expensive line, cost ten francs.

French, perhaps Pantin;
c. 1875–80.
Diameter: 11.5 cm.
Gift of the
Honorable Amory Houghton

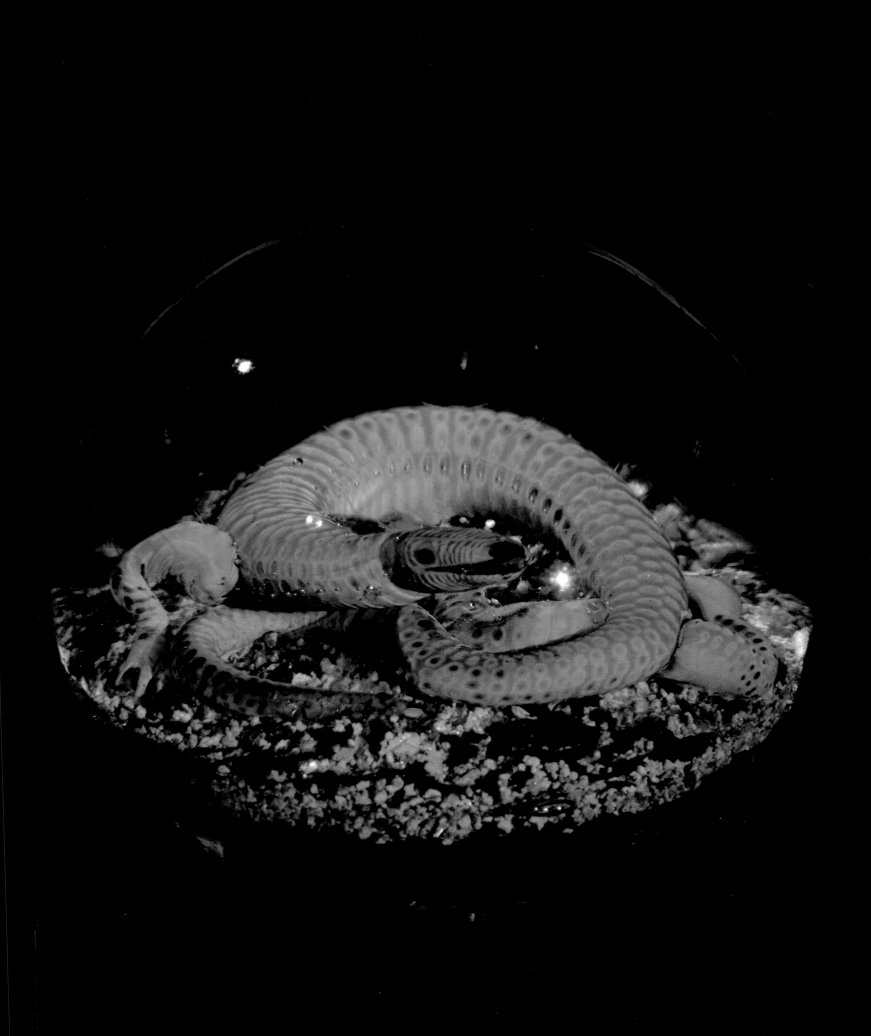

Ewer with Rock Crystal Engraving

From before the middle of the nineteenth century, Bohemian glass engravers had been tempted—no doubt by the prosperity of the Victorian era—to emigrate to England, where the craft of wheel engraving had never produced great practitioners. By 1875 a considerable number of these immigrant engravers were working in England, mainly at Stourbridge, and in Ireland. The two most influential glass firms in Stourbridge were Messrs. Thomas Webb and Sons and Messrs. Stevens and Williams Ltd. For the former worked Frederick E. Kny and William Fritsche (b. 1853, Meistersdorf; d. 1924, Stourbridge); for the latter, Joseph Keller.

At this time glass engraving in England was dominated stylistically by neoclassicism in its dying phase, an influence made explicit by the English glass engraver John Northwood in his straight copy of the Portland Vase and in his "Elgin Vase," finished in 1873, of clear glass with a zone of mounted figures in relief taken directly from the Parthenon frieze. In the same year Kny engraved his "Elgin claret jug" on exactly the same theme. This was also the year of the International Exhibition in Vienna, and in contemporary comments there is evidence of a shift of taste, noting "an infusion of Japanese art which is steadily moving into European design. . . . A third set . . . was rather more in Chinese than in Japanese style . . . framed upon the model of jade or rock crystal vases." This was a prophetic phrase, and comments on the Paris Exhibition of 1878 note, "Another development is that of deep, bright cutting, sometimes in relief, sometimes sunk." Henceforth, oriental motifs rendered in polished intaglio engraving, with relief cutting in convex forms, were to dominate glass decoration until the turn of the century.

The masterpiece in this genre was William Fritsche's ewer illustrated here, finished in 1886 after two-and-a-half years' work. Here oriental themes have been replaced by the watery motifs to which this kind of engraving was ideally suited. Its significance has to be read from the top downward in accordance with a program which was thoroughly Victorian in sentiment. "The whole ewer may be said to represent the progress of a river from its birth in a rocky hillside until it loses itself at last in the blue infinity of the sea. The neck of the ewer represents the mountain birth-place of the stream. . . . The rush and hurry of the rapid river are wonderfully expressed by the strong, clear, curving volutes of the body. . . . The lowest part . . . is formed of a great fluted shell . . . symbolic of the bottom of the sea. In this swim and sport a circle of vigorous dolphins. . . ." Despite all this, it is impossible not to discern in this magnificent object the clearest echoes from Fritsche's homeland. The alternation of broad convex polished cuts with minute wheel-engraved ornament was a characteristic of the Silesian glasses of the eighteenth century (no. 67); and the whole baroque power and rhythm of the composition call to mind the great seventeenth-century engraved rock crystals to be seen in central European collections.

Fritsche's ewer was sold directly to the U.S.A. in 1886, being bought by the New York jeweler Theodore Starr. It met with enthusiastic publicity, and was of great influence on the glasshouses and cutting shops of the United States in the succeeding decade.

English, Stourbridge; 1886. Height: 38.5 cm

Plaque Carved in the Cameo Technique

The first revival of cameo cutting on glass vessels since Roman times took place in England and was mainly the achievement of John Northwood (1836–1902), who had been apprenticed to the craft of enameling on glass in the famous glass-manufacturing firm of W. H., B. and J. Richardson of Wordsley, Stourbridge. The firm was dissolved when he was sixteen, and for a while Northwood learned carpentry with a brother until he rejoined the glass industry with Benjamin Richardson, a partner in the original firm and the most energetic and enterprising glassmaker in the district. Here Northwood showed his mechanical bent in collaboration on an etching machine, perfected about 1863, and made the acquaintance of some of the leading artistic personalities of the district. Benjamin Richardson was inspired by the notion of rivaling the masterpieces of the past by making a replica of the Portland Vase, and he offered an inducement of a thousand pounds to anybody who could bring off this feat. Northwood experimented and in about 1855 produced a blue cameo vase decorated with the subject of an Amazon attacked by a lion. In about 1862 he and his brother set up on their own in an etching workshop which in the 1860s and 1870s produced some of the best-etched work in the district, and he was now able to experiment further with the tools necessary to produce cameo glass. In 1873 he completed, after eight years' work, his "Elgin Vase" with a zone of figures in relief based on the Parthenon frieze (no. 91), the subsidiary classical ornament being acid etched.

The Portland Vase project was given further impetus by Philip Pargeter, a nephew of Benjamin Richardson and owner of the Red House Glassworks, near Stourbridge. The great difficulty lay in procuring blanks of a suitable quality, with a casing of opaque white glass over a dark blue ground; after many trials this was overcome, and by 1876 the replica was complete and aroused universal admiration.

John Northwood had had to devise his own tools for working on his cameo glass, and these took the form of steel burins cut to a long triangular point. The glass was put on a pad filled with bran and was carved. This method was obviously excessively laborious, and as cameo work spread in the Stourbridge district, acid etching and wheel engraving were called in to make the work easier. In 1876 John Northwood began work on the great Pegasus Vase, finishing it only in 1882 (now in the Smithsonian Institution, Washington, D.C.). Cameo glass now caught the public fancy, and the firm of J. and J. Northwood became in effect a decorating workshop of the leading glass enterprise of Stevens and Williams (no. 91), while the rival firm of Thomas Webb and Sons enlisted Thomas and George Woodall, themselves previously collaborators with John Northwood, to meet the demand.

The Woodalls, and their numerous helpers, turned out great quantities of cameo glass in the form of vases, dishes, scent flasks, and plaques decorated in white on grounds of a variety of colors, including a distinctive greenish beige. This quantity production led inevitably to a decline in quality and loss of favor with the public. The most ambitious pieces, however, were the large vases and plaques engraved by George Woodall himself, often assisted by his brother Thomas. These were usually decorated with vaguely classical themes, strongly sentimentalized in the late Victorian vein of Alma-Tadema and his contemporaries. The Corning plaque opposite is signed by George Woodall and was made during the 1890s. It shows Cupid with Venus (?) in a characteristic poolside setting.

English, Stourbridge;
c. 1895.
Diameter: 46 cm

94

Bowl with Colored and Wheel-engraved Decoration

Emile Gallé (1846–1904) may be considered as the artistic mainspring of the Art Nouveau movement in glass. He was the son of a furniture and faience manufacturer at Nancy, in eastern France, and he was therefore brought up in the atmosphere of an industrial establishment devoted to the applied arts. His father also made mirrors and table glass, however, and Emile Gallé himself was trained in the techniques of glass-making at Meisenthal, on the French-German border. By 1865 he was helping with the designing of glass and faience for his father's factories, and in 1867 he established his own glass-decorating workshop. Deeply inspired by Japanese art, then beginning to revolutionize European taste, and imbued with a fastidious love of nature, Gallé began to work out an entirely new style in glass.

Although at first he was not above copying earlier European forms and modes of decoration (using enameling and gilding, for instance), Gallé turned more and more to a style depending technically on the use of colored casings etched away and engraved to give poetic compositions of flowers and leaves with insects. In this technique he was no doubt guided by the example of Chinese cased and cut glass (no. 82), but he went far beyond his mentors in the complexity and subtlety of his relief effects, using a wider range of colors and base glasses, and supplementing the cased ornaments with wheel engraving, cutting, enameling, and gilding. To facilitate the work he was not afraid to make use of acid etching, which eats away the glass far more economically than it can be removed by manual methods. The initially crude effects of this technique were modified by the use of wheel cutting to modulate shapes and produce surface textures. By the time of the 1878 Paris Exhibition the production of art glass at the Gallé concern at Nancy had earned a reputation for quality and original invention.

The need to employ numerous assistants to sustain the high production of an industrial concern reduced progressively the artistic intervention of Gallé himself, and the personal character of the early glasses made before 1890 was gradually diluted. The extensive use of acid etching to produce cased floral designs against an opaque grayish white ground tended to produce a somewhat dead and monotonous effect. Many of the glasses, however, retained the freshness and originality that were the hallmarks of Gallé's earlier productions, and the bowl here embodies these qualities. It is decorated with embedded canes of yellow and white glass rising in S-shaped curves from base to rim in the grayish glass and cutting across the zone of purple at its base. The green disc foot stands in sharp contrast to this. The rim has been nipped in at three points, and below it is a frieze of dragonflies (a favorite motif with Gallé) wheel engraved with the utmost delicacy as a crowning refinement of this highly wrought glass. Amid the dragonflies the signature ''Gallé'' in rustic characters can be seen.

French, Nancy;
c. 1900.
Diameter (rim): 12.4 cm.
Bequest of Ellen D. Sharpe

95

Bowl in Pâte de Verre

Pâte de verre is regarded by some as hardly glass at all, for it is not made by methods normally used in a glasshouse. Nevertheless, the idea of shaping glass from a vitreous powder melted in a mold is probably one of the oldest techniques known in the making of glass (no. 6). The idea of producing glass in this way was revived in Europe toward the end of the nineteenth century by the sculptor Henri Cros (1840–1907). After experimentation in a special furnace at the Sèvres porcelain factory, Cros developed a suitable material with which to produce a series of sculptural reliefs, between the years 1892 and 1905. He had a number of disciples, including his son Jean, and Georges Despret (1862–1952), who was an important figure in the glass industry of his day, managing a glassworks at Boussois, but who made *pâte de verre* as a sideline and exhibited a number of small bowls at the Paris Exhibition of 1900, and thereafter extended his range in a series of small sculptures and other shapes.

By far the most important artistic figure in this movement, however, was Albert Dammouse (1848–1926), who trained as a sculptor, exhibiting in the Paris Salon of 1869, and then joined the staff at the Manufacture National de Porcelaine at Sèvres. Here he worked as a painter in the then fashionable Japanese taste, and later experimented with *pâte de verre* in a special kiln put at his disposal by the factory. From 1898 onward until his death he exhibited a series of small delicate bowls and vases, sometimes plain, but often decorated with floral and leaf ornaments in relief, in a palette of mostly pale colors that he had developed for himself. His unique style was refined and understated, and he had many admirers and imitators, including François Décorchement in Paris and members of the School of Nancy.

Pâte de verre is in some ways the antithesis of the general concept of glass, which is thought of as mainly transparent and always glossy. *Pâte de verre* was opaque or at best translucent, and its surface was usually somewhat matt and with a texture that betrayed its origins in a melting-together of tiny particles. These very features, however, combined with the subtlety of color of which it was capable, were responsible for a very special aesthetic appeal. This was something of which subsequent glass artists were to take full advantage.

French, Sèvres;
early 20th century.
Diameter: 11.1 cm.
Gift of James Barrelet

96

Favrile Vase with Iridescent Surface

As Emile Gallé dominated the latter part of the nineteenth century in European glass-making, so in America one man stood out above all the rest. This was Louis Comfort Tiffany (1848–1933), son of the creator of the great New York jewelry firm of Tiffany and Company. Louis Tiffany began his career as a painter, entering in 1866 the studio of George Inness, a well-known landscape painter influenced by the French Barbizon School. In the winter of 1868 he worked in the Paris studio of Léon Bailly, who interested him in the arts of the Near East. In the spring of 1869 Tiffany accordingly went to Spain and thence to North Africa in the company of a fellow American artist, Samuel Colman. On his return to the United States in 1870 Tiffany regularly contributed landscape and outdoor genre scenes, some inspired by his Near Eastern experiences, to exhibitions.

In 1871 Tiffany became an Associate of the National Academy, and in 1880 an Academician. In 1876, however, he exhibited nine paintings at the Philadelphia Centennial Exhibition, and here, through a connection with one of the judges, he became interested in the applied arts section, being particularly struck by the Japanese and English entries. Thereafter, with John La Farge he interested himself in stained-glass windows and began to study glassmaking techniques and chemistry at the Heidt factory in Brooklyn, the object being to make windows by the use of colors and leading alone. In 1879, with three kindred spirits including Samuel Colman he formed Louis C. Tiffany, Associated Artists, a firm devoted to a radical reform of all aspects of domestic interior decoration. In 1883 Mrs. Candace Wheeler, the textiles expert of the consortium, left the firm, and Tiffany, who in 1878 had established his own glasshouse in New York, formed the Tiffany Glass Company (1885), and turned increasingly to the design and production of glass windows, screens, and lighting fixtures. In 1889, however, he visited Europe, and probably saw in Paris Gallé's epoch-making contribution to the World Exhibition. In 1892 he reorganized his firm as the Tiffany Glass and Decorating Company, and a year later had his own furnaces at Corona making hollowwares under the supervision of Arthur J. Nash, an English glassblower of great talent and experience, with whom he worked in the closest collaboration.

Tiffany's vessel glass was something quite new. Although having some affinities with Gallé's work in its choice of motifs and its techniques of superimposing colored glasses, it differed in being virtually entirely furnace made, so that the ornaments inevitably reflected exactly the stages of working the parison. This produced sinuous flowing lines entirely in harmony with the Art Nouveau style, of which Tiffany was indeed the leading American exponent. In addition, his glasses were given an iridescent surface treatment by means of a process (patented in 1880) to produce a "metallic luster . . . by forming a film of a metal or its oxide . . . on or in the glass, either by exposing it to vapors or gases or by direct application." The idea of surface iridescence was not new, but Tiffany endowed it with a new quality and subtlety that raised it above the common level and gave it a surface "that was like skin to the touch, silky and delicate." By the combination of these technical elements under the influence of a refined and subtle taste Tiffany produced glasses of unequaled artistic quality.

The Corning vase illustrated here bears the mark "U 5099." It shows well the flowing lines of stem and leaf following the shape of the vase, and the subtle surface qualities of Tiffany glass.

American,
Corona, New York;
c. 1895–1905.
Height: 35.2 cm.
Gift of Edgar Kaufmann, Jr.

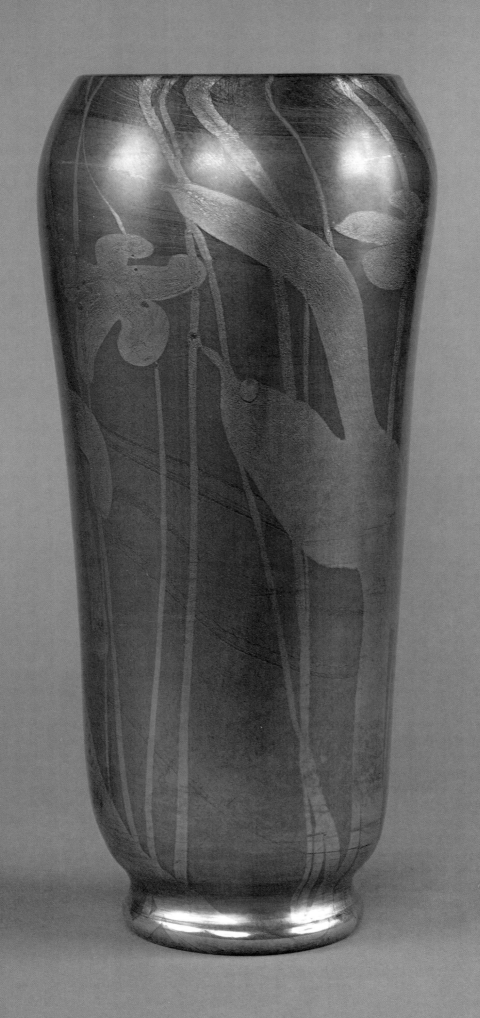

97

Intarsia Vase

Frederick Carder (1864–1963) was born at Wordsley, in Staffordshire, England. The son of a potter, he worked in the pottery business as a boy, but studied at the Stourbridge School of Arts to develop his artistic talents and for his technical training went to nearby Dudley, where he learned chemistry, electricity, and other natural sciences. Extraordinarily precocious at the age of seventeen, Carder joined the influential firm of Stevens and Williams at Brierley Hill, near Stourbridge, as a designer. This was the heyday of cameo glass (no. 92), and Carder produced work in this field that was worthy of comparison with the best (a fine plaque entitled *The Immortality of the Arts*, made in 1887, is in the Corning collection). In 1889 he was awarded gold and silver medals in a National Competition at South Kensington, London, against the competition of artists such as William Northwood, nephew of the great John Northwood and by six years Carder's senior.

For the next fourteen years Carder designed for Stevens and Williams, experimenting with many of the types of colored glasses then popular in England and on the Continent, which he visited in the course of business trips. These also took him to the United States, and contacts made during one of these visits led to his being invited to Corning in 1903 to set up the Steuben Glass Works. This project was financed by the Corning cutting firm of T. G. Hawkes & Co., and part of Steuben's business was to supply blanks to Hawkes for cutting. Steuben itself produced cut-glass and ''rock crystal'' engraving (no. 93), some of the cutting being executed on colored cased glasses, but this side of the business had less appeal for Carder than the production of colored glasses in the Art Nouveau style, particularly those with iridescent surface treatment and Tiffany-style inlaid designs. Carder made numerous inventions in this field, christening them with exotic names such as ''Aurene'' (iridescent glass in gold or blue, often with threaded and floral designs in the Tiffany manner), ''Marina'' blue, ''Pomona'' green, and so forth. Such names were frequently coined by the numerous American glasshouses that imitated Tiffany's productions and hoped to profit by giving them names to compete with Tiffany's ''Favrile.'' Carder was no mere imitator, however, and he had an astonishing range of techniques at his fingertips, including opalized effects, marbling (''Cluthra''), mica flecking, air traps, and acid etching, by which some coveted pastiches of Chinese cased and carved glasses were made. These technical changes were rung in an astonishing variety of colors.

Carder's protean character as technician and artist, however, produced no real style that could be called his own. Despite the technical ingenuity, the shapes were often stereotyped and lacking in vitality, their decoration often neither particularly harmonious nor calculated to bring the glass to life. With the glass illustrated here, however, his somewhat chameleonlike talent had a triumphant success. The vase is decorated in his inlaid ''Intarsia'' technique, and is clearly inspired by the ''Graal'' glasses evolved at Orrefors, in Sweden, from 1916 onward. Not only is the technique analogous, but the shape itself is one that would not look out of place in the Sweden of the 1920s. The flowing lines of Carder's design and the soft tones of color, those on one side overlapping and darkening those on the other, are of the essence of successful glass decoration.

American,
Corning, New York;
c. 1925.
Height: 17.5 cm.
Bequest of Gladys C. Welles

211

98

Vase with Molded Design Picked Out in Black

Starting his career as a jeweler, René Lalique (1860–1945) first made his name with his exquisite pendants, combs, and brooches at the Paris Exhibition of 1900. At the same time, however, he experimented with enamels and glass, at first as accessories in jewelry but then as the material of vessels, light fixtures, and windows. There is a curious parallel here with the artistic development of Louis C. Tiffany (no. 96), who at much the same time, in his capacity as art director and vice-president of Tiffany and Co., had produced many designs for the jewelry in mixed media which became fashionable toward 1900.

In 1908 Lalique acquired his own small glassworks at Combs-la-Ville, partly to meet an order from the house of Coty to produce special perfume flasks of high artistic quality to package particular scents in their product line. In 1918 he acquired a larger glasshouse at Wingen-sur-Moder. Lalique was in reaction against the colored and layered glasses of his predecessors in France, and virtually all his glass is made in clear or slightly opalized crystal (often with a faintly nacreous surface), in black, or in a single pale color that does not impair the translucency of the material. At first his glass was hand blown, but he did not shrink from the use of molding to make a series of identical glasses, a virtual necessity in the case of flacons for perfume. The idea was transferred to larger objects, often producing a great depth of relief, as in the vase illustrated. Lalique also sometimes used the *cire perdue* method for his more imposing individual pieces, on which he did not hesitate to use figural subjects in high relief in a conventional classical manner. Far more frequent, however, were his molded vases in which decorative elements—birds, plants, fish, or human figures—were rigorously disposed, often symmetrically, in sharply defined ornamental arrangements. The Corning vase, the design for which was probably made in 1925, shows well how the deep beveled design in frosty crystal is given smartness and sharpness by the surface application of opaque black, a touch entirely in character with the brittle, hard mood of the 1920s. The design was called "Tourbillons" ("Whirlwind" or "Whirlpool"), but its spiny curves are far more reminiscent of the unfolding of some thorny plant.

Lalique designed much glass for architectural purposes and for lighting, again calling to mind the example of Tiffany. He also made table- and stemware, the latter often with molded stems interposed between plain bowls and feet. The business survived World War II and continued under the direction of Lalique's son, Marc. René Lalique's direct influence on glass, however, was essentially a feature of the 1920s and 1930s, when it played a vital role in the formation of contemporary style.

French, Wingen-sur-Moder; c. 1925. Height: 20.4 cm

212

99

Acid-etched Vase

A unique phenomenon in his day, Maurice Marinot (1882–1960) has had no rival since. He was unique because he was the first artist to learn the whole craft of the glassmaker and was not a glassmaker aspiring to the higher realms of art. He began as a painter, entering the École des Beaux-Arts in Paris in 1901 and working in the studio of Fernand Cormon, a conventional painter who became intolerant of the radical views and revolutionary style of the nineteen-year-old Marinot. He was expelled from the studio but returned to take advantage of the models when the master's back was turned. In 1905 he returned to his native Troyes and never left it again for long. He exhibited regularly in Paris until 1913, being ranked among the Fauves and numbering André Derain, André Dunoyer de Segonzac, and André Mare among his friends.

In 1911 Marinot visited a glasshouse belonging to friends at Bar-sur-Seine, not far from Troyes. The sight of glassworking made an immediate impression on him, and he was captivated by the qualities of glass as a material. At first—naturally enough in a painter—he tried enameling. On shapes often made specially to his designs, he painted bright colors in a free, lighthearted vein that won him immediate acclaim. In 1914 a French critic, contrasting him with Albert Dammouse and René Lalique (nos. 95 and 98), wrote of him, "With M. Maurice Marinot, one returned to pure glass, transparent light glass, but adorned with joyous enamels, blues and reds, always vibrant. . . ." This superficial involvement with glass, however, did not long satisfy him. As he wrote in 1925, "The truth is that it is from inside a craft that one must create." Some years before this, already thirty years old, Marinot had started to study the glassmaker's craft and he learned, as he said, "with passion." His writings show that he understood well the forces that went into the making of a work of art in glass— the qualities of the material itself, the internal force of the expanding air meeting the outward force of the tools constraining it, the ever-present effects of gravity, and the fluctuating struggle between heat and cold. He saw reflected in his glass the forces of nature: "My aim [is]. . .to evoke at red-heat sinuous muscular responses which will then, after cooling, produce objects born of the fire to give the feeling . . . of water, still or flowing, of ice which is cracking and melting. . . ." The vision was perfectly matched by technique. He learned acid etching, using it in successive applications which suggested geological strata, and perfectly evoking the effects of melting ice, as can be seen here. He mastered the controlled production of bubbles in the glass, and produced color effects by trapping oxides below successive gathers of clear crystal. At the cutter's wheel he produced matt or polished facets and scoops that give the feeling of fractures in natural stones. Each new glass conjured up visions of others that might follow, and in the evening, after tiring hours at the furnace, he sketched incessantly, with seemingly inexhaustible invention, to record his ideas for future realization. In 1937, however, he was forced to abandon his glassmaking career because of the closure of the Bar-sur-Seine factory, and he returned to full-time painting.

Marinot's work may be said to lie at the root of almost all subsequent artistic glassmaking. When he appeared at the great Paris Exhibition of French Glass in 1951, he was introduced to the company as "Marinot, to whom you owe everything."

French, Bar-sur-Seine;
1934.
Height: 17 cm·
Gift of
Mademoiselle Florence Marinot

215

100

Wheel-cut and-engraved Covered Jar

From the beginning of its manufacture in the remotest epochs, there has been a dichotomy in people's attitude to glass. First valued as a substitute for natural hardstones, glass was seen to have also a life of its own, reaching its rigid, stonelike character by way of a plastic phase that obeyed other laws. Glassmakers have been grappling with this ambivalence ever since, and the dilemma was certainly not lessened when in due course they acquired the technical skill necessary to produce colorless glass that rivaled rock crystal itself. At different times of history one concept has dominated the other. In the Renaissance, Venetian glassmakers triumphantly asserted the glassiness of glass worked at the furnace (but nevertheless called their colorless glass *cristallo*). Almost at the same time, however, in the German lands, a concept of glass as nearly as possible resembling rock crystal was gaining the upper hand. The end in view was to apply to its embellishment the methods of wheel cutting and engraving that had been the only possible method of shaping and decorating natural crystal and other hardstones.

The exquisite wheel engraving of the seventeenth and eighteenth centuries was first supplemented and then virtually ousted by wheel cutting, which dominated the first half of the nineteenth century. But cutting became complicated and forfeited the light-enhancing virtues that had been its original aesthetic justification. The well-known result was the denunciation by John Ruskin in *The Stones of Venice* (1853), lauding the ductility and transparency of glass: "All work in glass is bad which does not, with loud voice, proclaim one or other of these qualities. Consequently, *all cut glass is barbarous*, for the cutting conceals its ductility and confuses it with crystal. . . ." Today Ruskin's end of the seesaw appears to be again in the ascendant.

In some quarters, however, the time-honored and aesthetically justifiable concept of glass as a stonelike material calling out for cutting and engraving is still sustained. Apart from the countries where these crafts have been favored by tradition, such as England and Bohemia, there are smaller but not unimportant centers. One of these is formed by the pupils and assistants of the late Wilhelm von Eiff (1890–1943), perhaps the greatest glass engraver of the interwar years. Mainly self-taught, he went through the commercial mill in Paris in his twenties, working in the decorating shop of Charles Michel. A short stay in Vienna in 1913 brought him into contact with Michael Powolny and Stephan Rath, the leading spirit in the Lobmeyr concern; this was a turning point in his career. He was already by this time a skilled engraver on both glass and hardstones, able to work in either intaglio or relief. After war service he returned to Stuttgart, finally in 1922 becoming a professor in the Stuttgarter Kunstgewerbeschule. Here, apart from developing his own artistic skills, he taught and inspired a series of pupils and assistants who have kept alive the tradition of his work: Konrad Habermeier; Hans Klein; Eugen Hassenfratz; Hanns Model; Nora Ortlieb, who engraved the jar shown here; Åse Voss Schrader and Koso Kagami, who took von Eiff's ideas to Denmark and Japan; Helen Monro-Turner, who through the Juniper Workshop in Scotland has transmitted them to a further generation of glass decorators. Nora Ortlieb's jar, both in its shape and its softly modulated ridges flowing like drapery and textured with vertical cuts, is in the direct line of succession from von Eiff's glasses with relief-cut designs against matted grounds.

German, Stuttgart;
c. 1958.
Height: 21.5 cm

101

Cut Crystal Bottle with Color Enclosures

Despite the lead given by Maurice Marinot as an individual artist-craftsman (no. 99), the main impetus behind the creation of a new glass style in Europe after World War I may be said to have come from Sweden. At Orrefors, a then little-known glasshouse in the middle of the forest glassmaking area of Småland, in southern Sweden, it was decided in 1915 to engage as designer for the factory an artist who had made his mark in a totally different field. This man was Simon Gate (1883–1945), who had had conventional art training at the Academy in Stockholm. He was followed in 1917 by Edward Hald, a man of the same age but of a very different stamp, who had worked with Henri Matisse in Paris. They were employed to put new life into art glass in the Gallé manner which had begun at Orrefors shortly before Gate's engagement. During 1916 Gate, with Albert Ahlin, the manager, and Knut Bergqvist, the factory's most gifted master glassblower, worked out a new technique by which Gallé's colored reliefs were cased in crystal and thereby given a smooth surface and a new liveliness imparted by the subsequent working of the glass. This they called "Graal" glass.

Gate and Hald also turned their attention to the production of simple tablewares in the Functionalist spirit of the time, and to decorative glass, both colored and crystal, ornamented with wheel engraving. Gate's sumptuous classical manner was nicely balanced by the dry, witty, and much more modern style of Hald, and in due course a number of other gifted designers joined the Orrefors staff. The artist-designer concept quickly spread throughout the glassmaking district of Småland, and factories hitherto unknown in the field of artistic glass began to make a name. These included Reijmyre, Gullaskruf, Johansfors, Boda, and others, but particularly Kosta, the oldest established glassworks in the district, with a history going back to 1742. Glass in the Gallé manner had been made there since 1898 from designs by G. G. Wennerberg and Alf Wallander, but in 1917 the artistic direction passed to Edvin Ollers, also a painter, who introduced innovations there parallel with those of Gate and Hald. One technique in which Kosta developed a definite ascendancy was that of cutting. Some highly original intaglio cutting by Ewald Dahlskog in the late 1920s was followed by the development of a distinguished style of nonfigural cutting under Elis Bergh, director of design from 1929 until 1950. Bergh was succeeded by Vicke Lindstrand, an extremely versatile and original designer who had worked at Orrefors from 1928 and subsequently in the ceramics industry. Under his direction Kosta did distinguished work in all the fields in which Sweden had become renowned since 1916. He was joined in 1958 by Mona Morales-Schildt, who had designed for the ceramics factories of Gustavsberg and Arabia, and had been responsible for the decorative arts department of the great Stockholm store Nordiska Kompaniet. Her work, apart from designs for simple tableware and vases for everyday use, employs a combination of colored enclosures with cutting which is entirely in the Kosta tradition and which is aptly dubbed "Ventana" ("window" in Spanish). Her bottle of about 1960 shown here well exemplifies the clarity of outline, the clever use of color, and the simple but subtle visual effects of reflection and refraction which have distinguished modern Swedish glass.

Swedish, Kosta;
c. 1960.
Height: 10.2 cm

102

Vase with Colored Enclosures

Maurice Marinot was probably the first man in the Western world to undertake the making of glass single-handed (no. 99). When the glasshouse in which he worked closed down, however, he was constrained to return to painting. This situation in the world today has completely been transformed by the evolution of a type of small tank furnace which can be installed in a comparatively limited space and which suffices for the needs of a glassblower working by himself. Characteristically, this is an American invention, and its development is chiefly due to two people—Dominick Labino (b. 1910) and Harvey Littleton (b. 1922). Littleton, who had started as a potter and teacher of ceramics, was also familiar with the glass industry through family connections. Labino was a technician of great distinction in the glass industry and an inventor of many processes.

In March 1962 the Toledo Museum of Art in Ohio, invited Harvey Littleton to lead a seminar on glassworking. The group experimented with a small furnace which at first was inadequate to melt the glass materials used. With the assistance of Dominick Labino, this problem was overcome by means of a change in the materials used. A second seminar in June of the same year extended the range of technical possibilities offered by the new type of furnace, and thereafter each artist proceeded in his own way to utilize the invention in his own private workshop.

Littleton's work has been mainly sculptural in character, extroverted, energetic, and inventive of techniques to suit his current aesthetic purpose. Labino, who retired early from his employment in industry in order to devote himself exclusively to the personal manipulation of glass, has a natural bent toward glasses of relatively simple outline that embody decorative devices of technical refinement and subtlety. While Harvey Littleton is happy to bend to his needs any technique such as cutting, or the combination of glass with other materials, Dominick Labino's glass is essentially furnace worked. His sculptural forms are manipulated from hot glass, and the enclosures in his vases and purely decorative pieces are not cut or etched and then reheated and encased, but proceed entirely by the logic of the glassblower's craft. Supreme technical knowledge governs the happy combination of compatible glass materials and above all furnishes an unparalleled range of controlled colors.

From the work of these two artists, starting in 1962, stems the whole fruitful studio glass movement which is so powerful in the United States and which is gaining strength in many other countries.

The vase illustrated here shows within an outline of great simplicity two overlays of green glass of different tints, rising up in taut forms like the shoots of growing plants toward the lip, where a zone of pinkish orange, perfectly controlled, merges imperceptibly with the body color of the glass.

102
American,
Grand Rapids, Ohio;
1969.
Height : 16.5 cm

Glossary

alabastron (Greek): a small bottle or flask for perfume or toilet oil, usually with flat lip, narrow neck, cylindrical body, and two small side handles (no. 3)

amphoriskos (Greek): a toilet flask (*see* preceding item), usually of inverted pear shape and often tapering to a point or button foot (no. 4)

anneal: *see* lehr

a retortoli : *see lattimo*

aryballos (Greek): a toilet flask (*see* alabastron) of globular form with side handles

borsella (Italian): a tonglike tool used for shaping glass; the *borsella puntata* had a pattern on the jaws which was impressed on the glass

bow lathe: a lathe powered by the use of a bow, the thong of which was passed around the spindle of the lathe and rotated it as the bow was drawn backward and forward

cable: a pattern resembling the strands of a rope; or an applied glass thread of some thickness

cage cup (diatretum): a cup decorated by undercutting so that the surface design (usually a mesh ornament) stands free of the body of the glass, supported only by struts—thus giving the whole the appearance of an openwork cage (no. 20)

cameo: a style of cutting a layered glass (and originally the hardstones from which the glasses were copied) so that one color is carved to stand in relief against a ground of another color, usually white against a dark ground (no. 9)

cane: a rod of glass drawn out while softened and heated to a suitable degree of thinness

cased glass: a glass of one color covered with glass of another color. This can be done either by blowing the parison into an already prepared "cup" of the contrasting color or by dipping it into a pot containing the contrasting color and making a gather to cover it.

celery handle: a handle with vertical ribbing, usually used on Roman glass

cire perdue (French): a method of casting molten glass or metal. A layer of wax is laid over the internal form and shaped as necessary, and the external part of the mold is built up over the wax, which is then melted away. The resultant cavity is filled with molten metal, or, in the case of glass, with powder or small fragments which are melted down by prolonged heating.

claw beaker: a beaker decorated with normally superimposed rows of hollow trunk-like "claws" (no. 22)

cobalt: a metallic chemical element used as the source of blue colorants in glassmaking. The raw material supplied was usually in the form of zaffer, an impure oxide of cobalt. This very intense colorant was usually diluted by fusing with potassium carbonate and a silicate to make smalt, which was in turn used to color glass blue (no. 75).

cone beaker: a drinking vessel in the shape of a tall slender cone, usually with trailed thread decoration (no. 21)

core technique: the earliest method of making hollow glass vessels, in which a core made of clay with organic binders was affixed to the end of a metal rod and used as the internal form on which to model the vessel (nos. 1, 3, 4)

cristallo (Italian): a term used for Venetian glass that as nearly as possible resembled rock crystal (that is, colorless and transparent), although most glasses to which the term was applied had in fact a tinge of brown or gray

crizzling: *see* glass disease

cup plate: a small plate used to accommodate a tea or coffee cup when a person was drinking from the saucer

cut glass: glass abraded by pressing it against a rotating wheel either of stone or of iron fed with an abrasive powder; cut designs are usually executed in simple flutes or facets arranged in nonfigural abstract patterns

diatretarii (Latin): a group of artisans distinguished in certain Roman legal documents from *vitrearii* ("glassblowers"), as finishers of glass vessels by abrasive techniques (cutting and engraving)

die-sinker: a metal mold-maker

enamel: a glass, opaque or transparent, fusing at a relatively low temperature. It is usually employed in powdered form to decorate the surface of metalwork, pottery, or glass, and requires a lower melting point than the material on which it is used. It is usually compounded with a medium, such as oil of lavender, to facilitate painting; this vehicle is burned away when the object is fired to fix the enamel.

eye beads: beads that are decorated with applied or embedded circular motifs resembling an eye

façon de Venise: a term describing glass made in the Venetian manner, or of Venetian-type material, in centers other than Venice itself

"Favrile": a type of glass patented by L.C. Tiffany in 1894, its distinguishing feature being an iridescent surface coating

feather or festoon patterns: variations of applied thread decoration, where the spirally applied thread has been drawn upward with a point in vertical lines, to give a series of hanging loops or festoons; or alternately upward and downward to give a feather pattern

fire polish: a finish given to the surface of a glass which by being worked has lost some of its surface smoothness; this can be restored by resubmitting the glass to the heat of the furnace, often at an aperture (glory hole) made specially for the purpose of reheating (no. 12)

flashing: superimposing a thin layer of glass on a parison of a different color or type, by dipping the parison in a pot of the second glass (sometimes also called "casing")

flux: a chemical substance used to lower the melting point of the main silica constituent of the glass material (e.g., soda, potash, lead)

forest glass: glass (usually green) made in the forest glasshouses (of the Middle Ages and later) in central and northern Europe. These glasses were usually fluxed with potash derived from the wood with which the furnaces were fueled; they derived their green tones from the iron impurities in the sands available.

gaffer: English word (corruption of "grandfather") describing a Master, or leader of a "chair" or team of glassworkers, as it was of a foreman in many other types of enterprise

gather: *see* parison

glass disease: a defect (not infectious) of a glass which loses its durability owing to imbalance among the oxides which constitute it (usually an unduly high alkali or too little lime). This tends to show itself in surface moisture, a fissuring of the body in fine gleaming lines (crizzling), and a surface dulling. If the condition is not checked, the glass will eventually disintegrate.

glass pincher: a workman who makes small objects (e.g., buttons or chandelier parts) by "pinching" a small quantity of malleable glass between the shaped jaws of a pair of tongs

glory hole: *see* fire polish

gold-band glasses: glasses decorated with ribbons of gold leaf, usually "shattered" by expansion, embedded in a transparent glass matrix (no. 10)

"Graal" glass: a type of glass evolved in the Orrefors glasshouse (Sweden), decorated by means of cut or etched designs in a colored layer of glass over the original parison, the whole being then reheated and covered with a flashing of colorless glass

head beads: beads (usually fairly large) made in the form of heads, the features of the faces, etc. formed in contrasting colors of opaque glass, probably at the lamp

Hochschnitt (German): relief cutting or engraving

Hofkellereigläser (German): glasses supplied for use in the buttery of a German court, the term being particularly used of enameled glasses

hookah (Arabic): a type of water pipe used in the East (no. 65)

Humpen (German): a large beaker of cylindrical form, usually in enameled glass

hyalos (Greek): glass in its translucent and colorless aspects

ice-glass: a type of glass (usually colorless) decorated by dipping the hot parison into cold water, thus fissuring the surface, which could then be reheated to restore its smoothness

intaglio (Italian): a method of engraving by which the decoration is cut into the substance of the glass (or stone) and lies beneath the plane of its surface

Intarsia (Italian): normally a woodworker's term, borrowed to describe a type of glass elaborated by Frederick Carder, in which a design of colored glass applied to the outside of a colorless parison was itself covered by a flashing of crystal glass (no. 97)

kantharos (Greek): a drinking cup of roughly bell shape, standing on a foot, with a pair of side handles

knop: a knob of glass, usually used in the stem or cover finial of a wineglass. Knops can be of a number of shapes: annulated knops, bladed knops, etc.

Kuttrolf (German): a flask with a neck divided into a number of tubes, found in German glass of the late Middle Ages and later and in Venetian and *façon de Venise* glass in the sixteenth to seventeenth centuries (no. 42)

lacy glass: a type of mold-pressed glass in which the whole surface is covered with ornament, the main motifs being set on a diaper ground of dots

lampwork: glass made by manipulating rods and tubes in the flame of a lamp or burner brought to an intense heat by the use of bellows or the like (no. 73)

lattimo (Italian): a word derived from *latte* (Italian for "milk") to denote an opaque white glass, usually opacified by the use of tin oxide or arsenic. *Lattimo* glass was much used in the making of decorative canes. Single threads or collapsed tubes (*a fili*), or cable twists (*a retorti, a retortoli,* or *a filigrana*) could be used by themselves or combined with each other (nos. 40–41).

lead crystal: a clear colorless glass fluxed mainly by the use of lead oxide (about 20–30 percent of the total batch)

lehr (corrupted from Italian *l'era*): the chamber of a furnace in which the glass is gradually cooled after forming. This slow annealing process is essential to reduce strains in the glass.

lily-pad decoration: a gather of glass around the base of a vessel that has been drawn upward into four or more curved projections with rounded ends (no. 87)

lion-mask stem: a hollow stem made by blowing into a mold patterned with two lions' masks, usually with festoons between

lustred glass: glass decorated with metallic pigments developed in a reduction firing to show a slight iridescence. The most common is a yellow pigment based on silver.

Mamluk (Arabic, "a slave"): a mercenary, usually recruited from among the slave class, and forming part of the bodyguard of the ruler of Egypt. The Mamluks finally usurped power about 1250 and chose the sultans from among their own number.

marver (corruption of French *marbre,* "marble"): a smooth slab, originally of stone but in modern times usually of metal, on which the glass gather is rolled to smooth and consolidate it and to give it the desired shape

milled threading: decoration by means of an applied ribbon or thread of glass which has been closely notched either by the use of a runner like a roulette, or by repeated indentation using the edges of the *pucellas* (tongs)

millefiori (Italian, meaning "thousand flowers"): a decoration obtained by embedding in a glass matrix slices of decorative canes having flowerlike patterns in the cross section. The term is sometimes loosely applied to other sorts of mosaic glass (no. 8).

mirror monogram: a monogram written in such a way that each letter is reversed to produce its mirror image, the letter and its image being then combined to give a symmetrical ornamental form. Letters such as M and W, being symmetrical anyway, were used alone.

mold blowing: glass may be blown into a mold to produce a finished shape and pattern (no. 13) or into a mold with a simple pattern such as a mesh or vertical ribbing and then worked in such a way as to distort the pattern as the vessel is shaped (no. 63)

mold pressing: a process, essentially of the nineteenth century, in which a gob of glass was mechanically squeezed between two parts of a mold to impart both shape and pattern simultaneously

mosaic glass: glass ornamented by means of sections of patterned glass of various opaque colors laid side by side and embedded in a matrix, or themselves run together to form the body of the glass. The patterns may be formal and figural (no. 8), or abstract (no. 11).

mosque lamp: a somewhat misleading phrase used to describe what is usually the outer shell of a lamp used for the illumination of a mosque, the actual wick holder and oil reservoir probably having been suspended within it. The mosque lamp usually had three, or later six, loop handles for suspension by chains from the roof of the chamber.

Nuppenbecher (German): a beaker decorated with applied prunts, usually of the same green color as the base glass, and often drawn out into thornlike projections (nos. 48–49)

oenochoe (Greek): a jug with a tall loop handle, an ovoid body, a flat base or small foot, and usually a trefoil pouring lip

par(a)ison: a gather of glass, sometimes used to refer to a gather already incorporating the first bubble of inflation

pâte de verre (French): a glass made by melting down already powdered glass in a mold

potash-lime glass: glass material fluxed exclusively or mainly by means of potassium compounds and stabilized by the addition (deliberately or unconsciously) of a sufficient quantity of lime

prunt: a decorative pad of glass applied to the wall of a vessel, usually drawn out into a thornlike projection (nos. 48, 49) or stamped with a die producing a pattern of dots in relief ("strawberry" or "raspberry" prunts, no. 63)

pyxis (Greek): a covered box for the toilet table, normally of cylindrical shape, with a low domed cover

reducing atmosphere: a smoky atmosphere (deficient in oxygen) in a kiln or furnace, sometimes deliberately created to reduce oxides to their metallic state, as in the case of lustre pigments (*q.v.*)

refractory: a substance, normally a clay, capable of resisting a high temperature

rhyton (Greek): a drinking vessel, usually in the form of a human or animal head, made to be set down on its rim

ribbon glass: glass produced by a technique of combining strips of glass of different colors and kinds and fusing them to produce a vessel (nos. 10–11); also sometimes used of Venetian-style glass decorated with *lattimo* stripes

Roemer (German): a drinking glass formed of a flaring or ovoid bowl above a hollow cylindrical stem, both made from the same parison, the stem being set on a conical foot, often made of a single spirally wound thread. The stem is normally decorated with rows of applied prunts, and a thread is laid around the junction of stem and bowl (nos. 48–49).

Schwartzlot (German): a sepia enamel transferred from stained-glass painting and used for the decoration of vessel glass, sometimes by itself, sometimes combined with other colors or gold. Internal details of the painting are usually scratched on with a point.

skyphos (Greek): a cup standing on a low foot, with side handles

serpent stem: *see verres à serpents*

sepia enameling: *see Schwartzlot*

sick glass: *see* glass disease

"Silesian" stem: a misnomer used of a molded, usually ribbed, shouldered stem, made by blowing or pressing into a mold and drawing out the resultant parison. Most common in Thuringian glass, it was introduced into England and much used there probably from about 1715.

smalt: *see* cobalt

snake threads: threads applied in serpentine forms to the surface of a vessel, usually pressed flat and hatched or crosshatched by means of a tool made for the purpose. Snake threads can be either self-colored or in opaque colors contrasting with the glass of the vessel itself.

Spechter (German): a word of uncertain meaning, used of tall, narrow, green drinking glasses made in the Spessart area of Germany. This form is sometimes incorrectly identified with the *Stangenglas* (q.v.).

Stangenglas (German): *Stange* in German signifies a pole, and a *Stangenglas* is a tall, narrow cylindrical glass, usually standing on a pedestal foot

stickwork: the use of a point to etch out the internal details of enameled decoration (*see Schwartzlot*)

vermiculée design: a convoluted ground pattern, resembling the tracks of worms on sand

verre de Nevers (French): usually associated with the small lampworked figures of the eighteenth and nineteenth centuries made at Nevers (and elsewhere) in opaque colored glasses (no. 73). Many other types of glass, however, were also made at Nevers.

verre églomisé (French): glass (usually flat) decorated with etched gold or silver foil backed up by painting in cold colors, all this executed on the reverse of the glass.

verres à serpents (French): this term ("snake glasses") is taken to mean glasses with stems elaborately fashioned to resemble snakes or dragons (nos. 54–55)

Waldglas (German): *see* forest glass

zaffer: *see* cobalt

zuccarin (Italian): an Italian version of the German *Kuttrolf* (q.v.)

Bibliography

Amaya, Mario. *Tiffany Glass*. New York: Walker & Co., 1967.

Antiques Magazine. American Glass from the Pages of Antiques. Vol. I ed. Marvin D. Schwartz; vol. II ed. Robert E. DiBartolomeo. Princeton, New Jersey: Pyne Press, 1974–1975.

Arwas, Victor. *Glass: Art Nouveau to Art Deco*. New York: Rizzoli International Publications, 1978.

Auth, Susan H. *Ancient Glass at the Newark Museum*. Newark: Newark Museum, 1977.

Barrelet, James. *La verrerie en France de l'époque gallo-romaine nos jours*. Paris: Librairie Larousse, 1953.

Beard, Geoffrey. *International Modern Glass*. London: Barrie and Jenkins, 1976.

———. *Modern Glass*. London: Studio Vista, Dutton Pictureback, 1968.

Beck, Horace C. "Glass before 1500 B.C." *Ancient Egypt and the East*. December (1934): 7–21.

Bickerton, L. M. *An Illustrated Guide to Eighteenth-century English Drinking Glasses*. Bibliography of English glass by D. R. Elleray. South Brunswick and New York: Great Albion Books, 1972.

Blair, Dorothy. *A History of Glass in Japan*. Tokyo: Kodansha International and Corning Museum of Glass, 1973.

Bloch-Dermant, Janine. *L'art du verre en France, 1860–1914*. Edited by Denoël. Lausanne: 1974.

Blount, Berniece and Henry. *French Cameo Glass*. Des Moines, Iowa: Dr. and Mrs. Henry C. Blount, Jr., 1968.

Boesen, Gudmund. *Venetianske Glas på Rosenborg*. Text in Danish, Italian, English. Copenhagen: G.E.C. Gads Forlag, 1960.

Bröhan, Karl H. *Sammlung Bröhan. Kunst der Jahrhundertwende und der zwanziger Jahre*. Vol. II, *Kunsthandwerk, Jugenstil, Werkbund, Art Déco*, Part I: Glas, Holz, Keramik. Berlin: Sammlung Bröhan, 1976.

Buckley, Francis. *A History of Old English Glass*. London: E. Benn, 1925.

Buckley, Wilfred. *European Glass*. Boston and New York: Houghton Mifflin Co., 1926.

Chambon, Raymond. *L'histoire de la verrerie en Belgique du IIme siècle à nos jours*. Brussels: Librairie encyclopédique, 1955.

Charleston, R. J., and Archer, Michael. "Glass and Stained Glass." *The James A. de Rothschild Collection at Waddeson Manor*. Fribourg: Office du livre, The National Trust, 1977.

Coburg. Kunstsammlungen der Veste. *Coburger Glaspreis 1977 für moderne Glasgestaltung in Europa*. Coburg: Kunstsammlungen der Veste Coburg, 1977.

Cologne. Kunstgewerbemuseum der Stadt. *Glas* [von] Brigitte Klesse [und] Gisela Reineking-von Bock. Cologne: Kunstgewerbemuseum der Stadt, 1973.

———. *Sammlung Giorgio Silzer: Kunsthandwerk vom Jugendstil bis zum Art Déco*. Austellung vom 16.6–19.9. 1976. Cologne: Kunstgewerbemuseum der Stadt, 1976.

Corning Museum of Glass. *Glass Drinking Vessels from the Collections of Jerome Strauss and the Ruth Bryan Strauss Memorial Foundation: A Special Exhibition*. Corning, New York: Corning Museum of Glass, 1955.

———. *Glass from the Ancient World: The Ray Winfield Smith Collection*. Corning, New York: Corning Museum of Glass, 1957.

———. *Glass from the Corning Museum of Glass: A Guide to the Collections*. Corning, New York: Corning Museum of Glass, 1958; rev., 1965, 1974.

———. *New Glass: A Worldwide Survey*. Corning, New York: Corning Museum of Glass, 1979.

———. *Paperweights: "Flowers which clothe the meadows."* Corning, New York: Corning Museum of Glass, 1978.

———. *A Survey of Glassmaking from Ancient Egypt to the Present*. Chicago: University of Chicago Press, 1977. Textfiche.

———. *Three Great Centuries of Venetian Glass. A Special Exhibition*. Corning, New York: Corning Museum of Glass, 1958.

Crafts Advisory Committee. *Working with Hot Glass; Papers from the International Glass Conference; September, 1976*. London: the Committee, 1977.

Darmstadt. Hessisches Landesmuseum. *Glaskunst im Bann der Farbe.: I. Arte nova-Techniken der Glashütte, 1976. II. Vor der Lampe geblasenes Glas, 1978*.

Daverio, Paul J. *Louis Comfort Tiffany*. Lausanne: Galerie des Art Décoratifs, 1974.

Davis, Frank. *Early 18th-century English Glass*. London: Hamlyn Publishing Group, 1971.

Dillon, Edward. *Glass*. London: Methuen & Co., 1907.

Dimand, Maurice S. *A Handbook of Muhammadan Art*. New York: Metropolitan Museum of Art, 1944.

Doppelfeld, Otto. *Römisches und fränkisches Glas in Köln*. Cologne: Greven, 1966.

Düsseldorf. Kunstmuseum. *Glas, Band 1*. Bearbeitet von Elfriede Heinemeyer. Düsseldorf: Kunstmuseum, 1966.

————. *Glas, Band 3. Glassammlung Hentrick, Antike und Islam*. Axel von Saldern. Düsseldorf: Kunstmuseum, 1974.

————. *Glas, Band 5: Ausgewählte Werke*. Düsseldorf: Kunstmuseum, 1976.

————. *Leerdam Unica: 50 Jahre modernes niederlandisches Glas*. Exhibition. Kunstmuseum, 1977.

Eisen, Gustavus A., assisted by Fahim Kouchakji. *Glass*. 2 vols. New York: William E. Rudge, 1927.

Elville, E. M. *The Collector's Dictionary of Glass*. London: Country Life, 1961.

Farrar, Estelle Sinclaire, and Spillman, Jane Shadel. *The Complete Cut and Engraved Glass of Corning*. New York: Crown Publishers, 1979.

Flavell, Ray, and Smale, Claude. *Studio Glassmaking*. New York: Van Nostrand Reinhold Co., 1974.

Fossing, Poul. *Glass Vessels before Glass-Blowing*. Copenhagen: E. Munksgaard, 1940.

Frankfurt am Main. Museum für Kunsthandwerk. *Europäisches und aussereuropäisches Glas / Museum für Kunsthandwerk*. Frankfurt am Main: Museum für Kunsthandwerk, 1973.

————. *Europäisches und aussereuropäisches Glas*. C. und M. Pfoh-Stiftung / Museum für Kunsthandwerk. Frankfurt am Main: Museum für Kunsthandwerk, 1975.

————. *Modernes Glas aus Amerika, Europa und Japan / Ausstellung*. May 15–June 27, 1976. Frankfurt am Main: Museum für Kunsthandwerk, 1976.

Fremersdorf, Fritz. *Römische Gläser aus Köln*. Cologne: Verlags-Anstalt und Druckerei, 1928.

Frothingham, Alice Wilson. *Spanish Glass*. New York: Thomas Yoseloff, 1964.

Fukai, Shinji. *Persian Glass*. New York: John Weatherhill, 1977.

Gardner, Paul. *American Glass*. Washington, D. C.: Smithsonian Institution, 1977.

Gardner, Paul F. *The Glass of Frederick Carder*. New York: Crown Publishers, 1971.

Garner, Philippe. *Emile Gallé*. New York: Rizzoli International Publications, 1976.

Gasparetto, Astone. *Il vetro di Murano dalle origini ad oggi*. Venice: Neri Pozza Editore, 1958.

Gelder, H. E. van. *Glas en Ceramiek*. Utrecht: W. de Haan, 1955.

Godfrey, Eleanor S. *The Development of English Glassmaking, 1560–1640*. Chicago: University of Chicago Press, 1957.

Goethert-Polaschek, Von Karin. *Katalog der römischen Gläser des Rheinischen Landesmuseums Trier*. Mainz am Rhein: Verlag Philipp von Zabern, 1977.

Grover, Ray and Lee. *Art Glass Nouveau*. Rutland, Vermont: Charles E. Tuttle Co., 1967.

————. *Carved and Decorated European Art Glass*. Rutland, Vermont: Charles E. Tuttle Co., 1970.

————. *Contemporary Art Glass*. New York: Crown Publishers, 1975.

Guttery, D. R. *From Broad-Glass to Cut Crystal*. London: Leonard Hill, 1956.

Hald, Arthur. *Simon Gate, Edward Hald*. Stockholm: Norstedts, 1948.

Harden, Donald B. "Ancient Glass, I: Pre-Roman." *Archaeological Journal*, 125 (1969): 46–72.

————. "Ancient Glass, II: Roman." *Archaeological Journal*, 126 (1970): 44–77.

————. "Ancient Glass, III: Post Roman." *Archaeological Journal*, 128 (1972): 78–117.

————. *Roman Glass from Karanis*. Ann Arbor: University of Michigan Press, 1936.

————; Painter, K. S.; Pinder-Wilson, R.S.; and Tait, Hugh. *Masterpieces of Glass*. London: Trustees of the British Museum, 1968.

Hartshorne, Albert. *Old English Glasses*. London and New York: E. Arnold, 1897.

Hayes, John. *Roman and Pre-Roman Glass in the Royal Ontario Museum*. Toronto: Royal Ontario Museum, 1975.

Haynes, E. Barrington. *Glass Through the Ages*. Baltimore: Penguin Books, 1969.

Hetteš, Karel. *Old Venetian Glass*. Translated by Ota Vojtisek. London: Spring Books, 1960.

Hilschenz, Helga. *Das Glas des Jugendstils: Katalog der Sammlung Hentrich im Kunstmuseum Düsseldorf*. Munich: Prestel-Verlag, 1973.

History in Glass. London: Arthur Churchill, 1937.

Honey, William B. "Chinese Glass." *Transactions of the Oriental Ceramic Society*, 17 (1939/40): 35–47.

————. "Early Chinese Glass." *Burlington Magazine*, 71, no. 416 (1937): 211–22.

————. *Glass, A Handbook for the Study of Glass Vessels of All Periods and Countries and a Guide to the Museum Collections* (Victoria and Albert Museum). London: Ministry of Education, 1946.

Hughes, G. Bernard. *English, Scottish and Irish Table Glass from the Sixteenth Century to 1820.* London: B. T. Batsford, 1956.

Innes, Lowell. *Pittsburgh Glass, 1797–1891; A History and Guide for Collectors.* Boston: Houghton Mifflin Co., 1976.

Isings, Clasina. *Roman Glass from Dated Finds.* Groningen and Djakarta: J. B. Wolters, 1957.

Janneau, Guillaume. *Modern Glass.* London: The Studio, 1931.

Kämpfer, Fritz, and Beyer, Klaus G. *Glass: A World History, The Story of 4000 Years of Fine Glass-Making.* Translated and revised by Edmund Launert. London: Studio Vista, 1966.

Kato, Koji. *Glassware of the Edo Period.* Translated by Fumio Tanaka. Tokyo: Tokuma Shoten Publishing Co., 1972.

Kisa, Anton. *Das Glas im Altertume.* 3 vols. Leipzig: K. W. Hiersemann, 1908.

Koch, Robert. *Louis C. Tiffany, Rebel in Glass.* New York: Crown Publishers, 1964.

Kulasiewicz, Frank. *Glassblowing: The Technique of Free-blown Glass.* New York: Watson-Guptill Publications, 1974.

Labino, Dominick. *Visual Art in Glass.* Dubuque, Iowa: William C. Brown Co., 1968.

Lalique par Lalique. Compiled by Marc and Marie-Claude Lalique. Paris: Société Lalique, 1977.

Lamm, Carl J. *Glass from Iran in the National Museum, Stockholm.* Stockholm: C. E. Fritze, 1935.

————. "Glass and Hard Stone Vessels." In A. U. Pope, ed., *A Survey of Persian Art from Prehistoric Times to the Present,* 3:2592–606, 6:1438–55. London and New York: Oxford University Press, 1939.

————. *Mittelalterliche Gläser und Steinschnittarbeiten aus dem Nahen Osten.* 2 vols. Berlin: D. Reimer, 1929 and 1930.

Larsen, Alfred. *Dansk Glass 1825–1925.* 2nd rev. ed. Copenhagen: Nyt Nordisk Forlag Arnold Busck, 1974.

Lesieutre, Alain. *The Spirit and Splendor of Art Deco.* New York: Two Continents, 1974.

Littleton, Harvey K. *Glassblowing—A Search for Form.* New York: Van Nostrand Reinhold Co., 1972.

Lynggaard, Finn. *Glas Håndbogen.* Copenhagen: J. Fr. Clausens Forlag, 1975.

McClinton, Katharine Morrison. *Art Deco.* New York: Clarkson N. Potter, 1972.

McKearin, George S. and Helen. *American Glass.* New York: Crown Publishers, 1948.

————. *Two Hundred Years of American Blown Glass.* Rev. ed. New York: Bonanza Books, Crown Publishers, 1950.

McKearin, Helen. *The Story of American Historical Flasks.* Corning, New York: Corning Museum of Glass, 1953.

McKearin, Helen, and Wilson, Kenneth M. *American Bottles and Flasks and Their Ancestry.* New York: Crown Publishers, 1978.

Mainz. Mittelrheinisches Landesmuseum. *Jugendstilglas: Sammlung H. R. Gruber.* Text, Wolfgang Venzmer. Mainz: Mittelrheinisches Landesmuseum, 1976. (Abteilungskatalog 1)

Mariacher, Giovanni. *Italian Blown Glass from Ancient Rome to Venice.* London: Thames and Hudson, 1961.

Meyer-Heisig, Erich. *Der Nürnberger Glasschnitt des 17. Jahrhunderts.* Nuremberg: Verlag Nürnberger Press, 1963.

Mollica, Peter. *Stained Glass Primer.* Berkeley, California: Mollica Stained Glass Press, 1973.

————. *Stained Glass Primer, vol. II.* Berkeley, California: Mollica Stained Glass Press, 1977.

Morin-Jean. *La Verrerie en Gaule sous L'Empire Romain.* Paris: H. Laurens, 1913.

Neustadt, Egon. *The Lamps of Tiffany.* New York: Fairfield Press, 1970.

Neuwirth, Waltraud. *Das Glas des Jugendstils.* Munich: Prestel-Verlag, 1973.

Newman, Harold. *An Illustrated Dictionary of Glass.* With an introductory survey of glassmaking by Robert J. Charleston. London: Thames and Hudson, 1977.

Norman, Barbara. *Engraving and Decorating Glass.* New York: McGraw-Hill, 1972.

Oppenheim, A. Leo; Brill, Robert H.; Barag, Dan; and von Saldern, Axel. *Glass and Glassmaking in Ancient Mesopotamia.* Corning, New York: Corning Museum of Glass, 1970.

Papert, Emma. *The Illustrated Guide to American Glass.* New York: Hawthorn Books, 1972.

Pazaurek, Gustav E. *Kunstgläser der Gegenwart.* Leipzig: Klinkhardt & Biermann, 1925.

————. *Moderne Gläser.* Leipzig: Hermann Seeman Nachfolger, 1901.

Pazaurek, Gustav E., and von Philippovich, Eugen. *Gläser der Empire und Biedermeierzeit.* Braunschweig: Klinkhardt Biermann, 1976.

Pellatt, Apsley. *Curiosities of Glassmaking.* London: David Bogue, 1849.

Percy, Christopher Vane. *The Glass of Lalique.* New York: Charles Scribner's Sons, 1978.

Perrot, Paul N.; Gardner, Paul; and Plaut, James. *Steuben: Seventy Years of American Glassmaking.* New York: Praeger Publishers, 1974.

Pešatová, Zuzana. *Bohemian Engraved Glass.* Translated by Arnost Jappel. Prague: Artia for Paul Hamlyn, 1968.

Polak, Ada B. *Gammelt norsk glass.* English summary. Oslo: Gyldendal Norsk Forlag, 1953.

————. *Glass: Its Makers and Its Public.* New York: G.P. Putnam's Sons, 1975.

————. *Modern Glass.* New York: Thomas Yoseloff, 1962.

Powell, Harry J. *Glassmaking in England.* Cambridge: Cambridge University Press, 1923.

Rademacher, Franz. *Die deutschen Gläser des Mittelalters.* Berlin: Verlag für Kunstwissenschaft, 1933.

Revi, Albert C. *American Art Nouveau Glass.* Camden, New Jersey: Thomas Nelson & Sons, 1968.

————. *American Pressed Glass and Figure Bottles.* New York: Thomas Nelson & Sons, 1964.

————. *Nineteenth Century Glass, Its Genesis and Development.* Rev. ed. New York: Thomas Nelson & Sons, 1967.

Riefstahl, Elizabeth. *Ancient Egyptian Glass and Glazes in the Brooklyn Museum.* Brooklyn: Brooklyn Museum, 1968.

Rose, James H. *The Story of American Pressed Glass of the Lacy Period, 1825–1850.* Corning, New York: Corning Museum of Glass, 1954.

Saldern, Axel von. *German Enameled Glass.* Corning, New York: Corning Museum of Glass, 1965.

————. *Gläser der Antike, Sammlung Erwin Oppenländer.* Mainz: P. von Zabern, 1974.

————. *Glassammlung Hentrick, Antike und Islam.* Düsseldorf: Kunstmuseum, 1974.

Schlosser, Ignatz. *Das alte Glas.* 3rd edition. Braunschweig: Klinkhardt & Biermann, 1977.

Schmidt, Robert. *Brandenburgische Gläser.* Berlin: Verlag für Kunstwissenschaft, 1914.

————. *Das Glas.* 2nd ed. Berlin: Walter de Gruyter & Co., 1922.

Seitz, Heribert. *Äldre Svenska Glas. . .* English summary. Stockholm: Nordiska Museets Handlingar 5, 1936.

Selle, Gert. *Jugendstil und Kunst-Industrie zur Ökonomie und Ästhetik des Kunstgewerbes um 1900.* Ravensburg: Otto Maier, 1974.

Spillman, Jane Shadel. *Glassmaking: America's First Industry.* Corning, New York: Corning Museum of Glass, 1976.

————, and Farrar, Estelle Sinclaire. *The Cut and Engraved Glass of Corning, 1868–1940.* Corning, New York: Corning Museum of Glass, 1977.

Stennett-Willson, Ronald. *Modern Glass.* New York: Van Nostrand Rheinhold Co., 1975.

Thorpe, W. A. *English Glass.* 3d ed. London: A. & C. Black, 1961.

————. *A History of English and Irish Glass.* 2 vols. London: Medici Society, 1929.

Toledo Museum of Art. *American Glass Now.* [Exhibition at seven museums, 11/4/72–5/5/74]. Toledo, Ohio: Museum of Art, 1972.

————. *Art in Glass: A Guide to the Glass Collections.* Toledo, Ohio: Museum of Art, 1969.

Trowbridge, Mary Luella. *Philological Studies in Ancient Glass.* Urbana: University of Illinois Press, 1930.

Vávra, Jaroslav R. *5000 Years of Glass-Making: The History of Glass.* Translated by I. R. Gottheiner. Prague: Artia, 1954.

Wakefield, Hugh. *Nineteenth Century British Glass.* New York: Thomas Yoseloff, 1961.

Warren, Phelps. *Irish Glass: The Age of Exuberance.* London: Faber and Faber, 1970.

Weiss, Gustav. *The Book of Glass.* Translated by Janet Seligman. New York: Praeger Publishers, 1971.

Westropp, M. S. Dudley. *Irish Glass. A History of Glassmaking in Ireland from the Sixteenth Century.* Rev. ed. with additional text and illustrations. Ed. Mary Boydell. Dublin: Allen Figgis, 1978.

Weyl, W. A. *Coloured Glasses.* Sheffield: Society of Glass Technology, 1976. (paperback reprint)

Wiet, Gaston. *Lampes et bouteilles en verre émaillé.* Cairo: Museum of Islamic Art, 1929.

Wills, Geoffrey. *English and Irish Glass.* London: Guinness Signatures, 1968.

————. *Victorian Glass.* London: G. Bell and Sons, 1976.

Wilson, Kenneth M. *New England Glass & Glassmaking.* New York: Thomas Y. Crowell Co., 1972.

Index

Numbers in italic refer to illustrations.

Acid-etched vase, *214*, 215
Acid etching, 15, 215
Adam, John, 179
Aegina (island), 31
Ahlin, Albert, 219
Alabastron with threaded decoration, *22*, 23
Aleppo, 80
Alexander Severus (emperor, Roman Empire), 55
Alexandria (Egypt), 31, 32, 35, 40
Alma-Tadema, Lawrence, 200

Amelung, Johann Friedrich, 184
Amelung beaker, 9, *185*
Amenophis II (pharaoh), 20
Amman, Jost, 111, 156
Amphoriskos, *18*, 19, 24, *25*
Angster, 100
Anthonisz., Cornélis, 91
Antikythera (island), 31
Antwerp (Belgium), 95
Arabs, glassmaking by, 13
Arezzo potteries, 43

Ariston, 43
Aristophanes, 28
Artas, 43, 44
Art Nouveau, 15, 204, 208, 211
Augustus (emperor, Roman Empire), 43

Baghdad (Iraq), 72
Baiae (Italy), 55
Bailly, Léon, 208
Baluster goblet of lead glass, 144, *145*
Barcelona (Spain), 103
Barovier, Angelo, 14
Beakers
    with checkered spiral-trail decoration, white
      enameling, and gilding, *106*, 107
    claw, Frankish, 60, *61*
    cone, Frankish, *58*, 59
    covered, engraved in intaglio and relief,
      140, *141*
    Imperial Eagle, 108, *109*
    painted in transparent enamels, 172, *173*
    snake-thread, 48, *49*
    Waldglas, 88, *89*
Beert, Osias, 96
Beilby family, 159
Benckert, Hermann, 156
Bergh, Elis, 219
Bergqvist, Knut, 219
Bewick, Thomas, 159
Biedermeier period, 15, 176
Biemann, Dominik, 175
Bigaglia, Pietro, 196
Blancourt, Haudicquer de, 163
Blue cut-glass bowls, *166*, 167
Boardman, James, 195
Boers, Sebastiaan, 131
Bohemia, 15, 119, 148, 176
Boston and Sandwich Glass Company, 195
Bottle(s)
    cut-crystal, with color enclosures, *218*, 219
    cut glass, 68, *69*
    diamond-engraved, *130*, 131
    enameled opaque white glass, 160, *161*
    with mold-blown decoration, *78*, 79
    relief-cut, Islamic, *70*, 71
Bowl(s)
    blue cut-glass, *166*, 167
    cast and cut glass, 28, *29*
    with colored and wheel-engraved decora-
      tion, 204, *205*
    cut, Hellenistic, *30*, 31
    cut with relief bosses, *66*, 67
    fruit or salad cut glass, on pressed foot,
      168, *169*
    lattimo, with enameled and gilt decora-
      tion, *86*, 87
    in *pâte de verre*, *206*, 207
    pillar-molded, 40, *41*
    relief cut, Islamic, 72, *73*

ribbon glass polychrome, *38*, 39
    wheel-engraved, 52, *53.*
    See also Sugar bowls
Bristol glass, 167
Brun, Sigismund, 183
Burgkamir, Hans, 108
Butts glass with white-striped and enameled
    decoration, *118*, 119
Byzantium (Constantinople; Istanbul, Tur-
    key), 13, 67

Cairo (Egypt), 83
Cam, John da la, 143
Cameo glass cup, *34*, 35
Cameo technique, plaque carved in, 200, *201*
Cameron, Charles ,179
Candlesticks, cut and wrought, 164, *165*
Canosa (Italy), 31
Caravaggio, Michelangelo da, 99
Carder, Frederick, 203, 211
Carl XI (king, Sweden), 128
Carli, Johann Anton, 115
Carpaccio, Vittore, 87
Carré, Jean, 95
"Cased" technique of glassmaking, 15
Cast and cut glass bowl, 28, *29*
Cast and cut vase, *26*, 27
Ch'ien Lung, 180
Chinese porcelain, 87, 180
Chou period (China), 180
Claw beaker, Frankish, 60, *61*
Cleve, Joos van, 91
Cobalt, 167
Colman, Samuel, 208
Cologne (Germany), 51, 112, 115
    gold-decorated goblet, 57
    snake-thread glass in, 48
Cone beaker, Frankish, *58*, 59
Core-formed Egyptian vase, *18*, 19
Corinth, glassmaking in, 13
Cormon, Fernand, 215
Corning Flint Glass Works, 203
Corning Museum of Glass, 9
Cristallo, 14, 96, 107, 143, 216
Cristallo cup, covered, *90*, 91
Cristallo goblet with enameled and gilt de-
    coration, 84, *85*
Crizzling (glass disease), 128, 143
Crockett, Benjamin, 184
Cros, Henri, 207
Crystal glass, 14–15
Cup, *cristallo*, covered, *90*, 91
Cut-crystal bottle with color enclosures, *218*,
    219
Cut and engraved goblet with silhouettes, *170*,
    171
Cut glass bottle, 68, *69*
Cut and wrought candlesticks, 164, *165*
Czechoslovakia, 139, 175

Dahlskog, Ewald, 219
Damascus (Syria), 80
Dammouse, Albert, 207
Daphne Vase, 9, *46*, 47
Despret, Georges, 207
Diamond-engraved bottle, *130*, 131
Diamonds, 120, 123, 124
Diamond-stippled wineglass, *154*, 155
Diatretarii (glass cutters), 13
Diderot, Denis, 11
 Encyclopédie, illus. from, *6*
Disch Kantharos, 9, *56*, 57
Dish(es)
 with diamond-point engraving, *122*, 123
 purple, engraved with diamond point, 120,
  121
 wheel-cut, *202*, 203
Drinking glass(es)
 Roemer, 112, *113*, *114*, 115
 with white-striped decoration, *98*, 99
Drinking horn, 59, 76, 77
Dura-Europos (Syria), 47, 48, 63, 64, 67

Eginton, W. R., 172
Egypt
 alabastron with threaded decoration, *22*, 23
 core-formed vase, *18*, 19
 drinking horn of lustred glass, 76, 77
 enameled and gilt mosque lamp, *82*, 83
 Fatimid period, 71, 75
 glass furnaces, 11
 under Greek domination, 31
 mosaic glass of, 32
 pharaoh's head in cast and retouched glass,
  20, *21*
Eighteenth Dynasty (Egypt), 19, 20, 23
Elgin claret jug, 199
Elgin Vase, 199, 200
Enameled glass, 47, 156, 159
 in Germany, 119
 gilt goblets, *158*, 159
 gilt mosque lamp, *82*, 83
 gilt opaque white ewer, *46*, 47
 gilt vase, 80, 81
 Humpen, 116, *117*
 hunt goblet, *110*, 111
 sepia (*Schwarzlot*), *114*, 115
 transparent, 172
 in Venice, 84
England, 15
 blue cut-glass bowls, *166*, 167
 Bohemian engravers in, 199
 candlesticks, 164, *165*
 enameling in, 159
 Frankish cone beaker, *58*, 59
 goblet in *façon de Venise*, *94*, 95
 Irish glass banned by, 168
 lead glass in, *142*, 143, 144, *145*
 wheel-engraved hookah base, *146*, 147

Engraving
 diamonds for, 120, 123, 124, 131, 155
 Hochschnitt, 75, *138*, 139
 techniques, 52
 by wheel, 52, 55, 135, 136, 147, 148, 150,
  152, 156, 175, 183, 184, 204, 216
Ennion, 43, 44
Ewer(s)
 enameled and gilt opaque white, *46*, 47
 mold-blown, *42*, 43, 79
 with rock crystal engraving, *198*, 199
 with threaded decoration, *50*, 51

Faber, Johann Ludwig, 156
Façon de Venise, *94*, 95, 96, 124, 128
Fatimid period (Egypt), 71, 75
"Favrile" vase with iridescent surface, 208,
 209
Flask(s)
 pint, mold-blown, 192, *193*
 spirit, with wheel-engraved and enamel-
  painted decoration, 156, *157*
Flegel, Georg, 127
Foscarini, Francesco, 87
Foster, J. P., 192
France
 acid-etched vase, *214*, 215
 bowl with colored and wheel-engraved
  decoration, 204, *205*
 Lalique, René, 212
 paperweights, 196
 verre de Nevers lampworked figure, *162*, 163
Franconia (Germany), 116
Frankish claw beaker, 60, *61*
Frankish cone beaker, *58*, 59
Franklin, William, 187
Frescobaldi, 80, 83
Fritsche, William, 199
Fritsche Ewer, 9, *198*, 199
Fruit bowl of cut-glass on pressed foot, 168,
 169
Furnaces, 11
Furniture, *178*, 179
Fustat (Egypt), 76

Gaffers (glassblowers), 11
Gallé, Emile, 204, 219
Gallo, Vincenzo Angelo dal, 120
Gate, Simon, 219
Germany
 American glassmaking and, 184
 beakers, *106*, 107, 108, *109*, 140, 141
 covered goblet with wheel-engraved
  decoration, 136, *137*
 enameled *Humpen*, 116, *117*
 enameling in, 111, 119, 156, 159, 172
 ewer, *50*, 51
 Frankish glassware, *58*, 59, 60, *61*
 Roemers, 112, *113*, *114*, 115

snake-thread glass in, 48
Gil, Pere, 103
Glassblowing
  in China, 180
  by Ennion, 43
  invention, 12, 24, 44
  Kuttrolf, 100, *101*
  patterned molds for, 79
  ribbing in, 60
  in Roman Empire, 51
Glass disease (crizzling), 128, 143
Glassmaking, history, 9–15
Goblet(s)
  baluster, of lead glass, 144, *145*
  cristallo, with enameled and gilt decoration, 84, *85*
  cut and engraved, with silhouettes, *170*, 171
  with cut, engraved, stained, and enameled decoration, 176, *177*
  cylindrical, Sasanian, *62*, 63
  enameled and gilt, *158*, 159
  English, in *façon de Venise*, *94*, 95
  engraved in relief (*Hochschnitt*), *138*, 139
  engraved on wheel, 152, *153*
  engraved on wheel with decorative threads, 148, *149*
  gold-decorated, with protective network, *56*, 57
  hunt, enameled, *110*, 111
  royal, 128, *129*
  serpent-stem, 124, *125*, *126*, 127
  with wheel-cut and -engraved decoration, 150, *151*
  with wheel-engraved decoration, 136, *137*
  with white-striped decoration, 96, *97*
Goette, Johann Wolfgang von, 171
Gold-band pyxis, 36, *37*
Gold-decorated goblet with protective network, *56*, 57
Gordion (Phrygia), 28
"Graal" glass, 219
Greece, 27
  Hellenistic cut bowl, *30*, 31
  Serapis cult and, 32
Greene, John, 143, 144
Green glass *Roemer*, 112, *113*
Greenwood, Cornelis, 155
Greenwood, Grans, 155
Gurgan (Iran), 72, 79
Gutturnium, 100

Haedy, Christopher, 167
Hald, Edward, 219
Hall, Stephen, 167
Han dynasty (China), 180
Hans Wessler plaque, 9, *134*, 135
al-Harawi, 72
Harold Hardrada (king, Norway), 60
Hasan (sultan, Egypt), 83

Haseldine, John, 159
Hawkes, Thomas G., 203
Heda, Willem Claesz., 112
Hedwig (saint), 75
Hedwig glass, *74*, 75
Heinrich I (duke, Silesia), 75
Hellenistic period
  cameo glass cup, *34*, 35
  cut bowl, *30*, 31
  gold-band pyxis, 36, *37*
  mosaic glass plaque, 32, *33*
Helmhack, Abraham, 156
Heming, Thomas, 167
Herakleia (Turkey), 35
Hermsdorf (Poland), 139
Herodotus, 32
Hills, Peter, 119
Hoare and Dailey (company), 203
Hochschnitt (relief cutting), 75, *138*, 139, 140
Hofkellereigläser, 119
Holland, 131, 152
Holy Roman Empire, 139
Hookah base, wheel-engraved, *146*, 147
Hoolaart, G. H., 155
Houghton, Amory, 203
Houghton, Amory, Jr., 203
Howell, James, 9
H. P. Sinclaire & Co., 203
Hrabanus Maurus, 11
  manuscript ("De Universo"), illus. from, *10*
Hughes (glassmaker), 167
Humpen, 108
  enameled, 116, *117*
Hunt and Sullivan (company), 203
Hunt goblet, enameled, *110*, 111

Imperial Eagle beaker, 108, *109*
Inghistera, 100
Inness, George, 208
Intaglio engraving, 52, 135, 140, *141*
Intarsia vase, *210*, 211
Iran. *See* Persia
Iraq, *70*, 71, 72
Ireland, 168, *169*, 195
Islamic glassmaking, 13
  relief-cut bottle, *70*, 71
  relief-cut bowl, 72, *73*
Israel, 44
Italy
  cristallo goblet with enameled and gilt decoration, 84, *85*
  glassblowing in, 44
  wheel-engraved souvenir bottles, 55
  See also Venice
Ithaca (island), 31

Jacobs, Tynnes, 112
Japan, 64, 67

Jars
  handled, with wheel-engraved and gilt decoration, *182*, 183
  wheel-cut and -engraved, covered, 216, *217*
Jarves, Deming, 195
Jason (glassblower), 43
Johnson, Jerom, 164
Juan, Antonio, 183
Jug with furnace-worked decoration, *190*, 191
Jung, Gustav, 128
Juvenal, 55

Kalf, Willem, 127
K'ang Hsi, 180
Keller, Joseph, 199
Ken-amun, 20
Kisa, Anton, 48
Kny, Frederick E., 199
Kopidlnansky, Jörg von, 84
Koran, 83
Kosta (company), 219
Kunckel, Johann, 148
Kungsholm glasshouse, 128
Kuttrolf of colorless glass with opaque white thread decoration, 100, *101*

Labino, Dominick, 221
La Farge, John, 208
Lalique, René, 212
Lamp, mosque, enameled and gilt, from Cairo, *82*, 83
Lattimo, 96, 100
Lattimo bowl with enameled and gilt decoration, 9, *86*, 87
Lattimo-threaded wineglass, 104, *105*
Lavater, Johann Casper, 171
Lead, 143, 144
Lebanon, 36
Lehmann, Caspar, 135, 136, 139
Lindstrand, Vicke, 219
Littleton, Harvey, 221
Lomonosov, M. V., 179
Louis C. Tiffany, Associated Artists, 208
Lustred glass, drinking horn, 76
Lysle, Anthony de, 95

Maiolica (pottery), 87
Malipiero, Pasquale, 87
Mamluk enameled and gilt vase, 80, *81*
Mansur Muhammed ben Ahmad al-Daqiqi, Abu, 72
Marinot, Maurice, 9–11, 215, 221
Mathesius, Johann, 88, 107, 111, 120
Medallion, portrait, wheel-engraved, *174*, 175
Meges, 43
Memphis (Egypt), 32
Menzel, Johann Sigismund, 171
Mesopotamia, 12, 24, 27, 32, 63
Michel, Charles, 216

Ming dynasty (China), 87, 180
Miotti family, 160
Miseroni, Ferdinand Eusebio, 139
Modena, Nicoletto Rosex da, 84
Mohn, Gottlob Samuel, 172
Mohn, Samuel, 172
Mold blowing, *78*, 79
Mold-blown pint flask, 192, *193*
Montague, Mary Wortley, 179
Mooleyset, Willem, 124
Morales-Schildt, Mona, 219
More, Stephen, 167
Morelli, Allesio, 144
Morgan Cup, *34*, 35
Mosaic glass plaque, 32, *33*
Mosque lamp, enameled and gilt, from Cairo, *82*, 83
Müller, Michael, 148
Murano (island), 14
al-Mu'tasim (caliph, Iraq), 72

Nash, Arthur J., 208
al-Nāsir Yusuf II, 80
Neikaios, 43
Neikon, 43
Neri, Antonio, 183
Nero (emperor, Roman Empire), 39, 55
Netherlands, 131, 152
Nevers (France), 163
New York State, 191
Niebuhr, Carsten, 147
Nolpe, Peter, 124
Northwood, John, 199, 200
Northwood, William, 211
Nuppenbecher, 112
Nuremberg (Germany), 136

O. F. Egginton Company, 203
Ollers, Edwin, 219
Opaque white glass, 160, *161*
Ortlieb, Nora, 216

Paperweight enclosing figure of salamander, 196, *197*
Pargeter, Philip, 200
Pâte de verre, bowl in, *206*, 207
Paulo, Jeronimo, 103
Pearson, Eglinton Margaret, 172
Pearson, James, 172
Peckitt, William, 172
Pegasus Vase, 200
Péligot, Eugène, 196
Pellatt, Apsely, 195
Pencz, Georg, 135
Persepolis (Iran), 28
Persia (Iran), 13, 28, 31
  Islamic relief-cut bowl, 72, *73*
  lustred glass in, 76
  relief cutting of engravings in, 75.

See also Sasanian period
Pharaoh's head in cast and retouched glass, 20, *21*
Philip II (king, Spain), 104
Phoenicians, 24, 27
Phrygia, 28
Pillar-molded bowl, 40, *41*
Pitkin, William and Elisha, 192
Plaque(s)
    carved in cameo technique, 200, *201*
    crystal, wheel-engraved, *134*, 135
    mosaic glass, 32, *33*
Plate, pressed cake, *194*, 195
Pliny the Elder, 40, 43, 44
Poggibonsi, Ser Niccolo da, 80
Pohl family, 175
Poland, *74*, 75
Polychrome bowl, ribbon glass, *38*, 39
Populonia bottle, 9, *54*, 55
Porcelain, Chinese, 87, 180
Portland Vase, 13, 35, 199, 200
Portrait medallion, wheel-engraved, *174*, 175
Powolny, Michael, 216
Prague, 139, 175
Preissler, Daniel, 156
Preissler, Ignaz, 156
Pressed cake plate, *194*, 195
Ptolemaic dynasty (Egypt), 31, 32, 35
Ptolemy I (pharaoh), 32
Puteoli (Pozzuoli, Italy), 55
Pyxis, gold-band, 36, *37*

Ramos, Felix, 183
Rath, Stephan, 216
Ravenscroft, George, 14, 143, 144
Ravenscroft pieces, 9
Reinier, Jean Guillaume, 128
Relief-cut bottle, Islamic, *70*, 71
Relief-cut bowl, Islamic, 72, *73*
Rembold, Matthäus, 116
Ribbon glass polychrome bowl, *38*, 39
Ricci, Matteo, 180
Richardson, Benjamin, 200
Ricketts (company), 192
Robart, Willem Otto, 152
Rochefoucauld, Duc de la, 168
Rodriguez, Juan, 104, *105*
Roemers
    green glass, 112, *113*
    lead-glass, *142*, 143
    with sepia (*Schwarzlot*) enameling, *114*, 115
Roman Empire
    drinking vessels, 39
    ewer of mold-blown glass, *42*, 43
    glassblowing in, 44, 51
    glass engraving in, 52
    glassmaking in, 12, 13
    pillar-molded bowl, 40, *41*

    snake-thread glass in, 48
    wheel-engraved souvenir bottles, *54*, 55
Royal covered goblet, 128, *129*
Rudolf II (emperor, Holy Roman Empire), 139
Ruskin, John, 216
Russia, 179

Saichu, Emir, 83
Salad bowl of cut glass on pressed foot, 168, 169
Samarra (Iraq), 71, 72
Sang family, 152
San Ildefonso (Spain), 183
Sargon II (king, Assyria), 27
Sargon Vase, 27
Sasanian period (Persia)
    bowl cut with relief bosses, *66*, 67
    cut glass bottle, 68, *69*
    cut glass vase, 64, *65*
    cylindrical goblet, *62*, 63
Savoy Vase, 167
Scapitta, Giacomo Bernardini, 128
Schaper, Johann, 115, 156
Schneider, Christian Gottfried, 150
Schouman, Aert, 155
Schurman, Maria van, 131
Schwanhardt, Georg, 135, 136
Schwarzlot enameling, *114*, 115
Schwinger, Hermann, 136
Serpent-stem goblets, 124, *125*, *126*, 127
Shawabti (glass figurine), 20
Sidon (Syria), 43, 44
Sigismund, Michael, 172
Silesia, 150
Silhouette, Étienne de, 171
Simeonis, Symon, 80
Sit, Ventura, 183
Smalt, 167
Snake-thread beaker, 48, *49*
Solis, Virgil, 111
Son, Georges von, 127
Souvenir bottle, *54*, 55
Spain
    enameled *tazza*, *102*, 103
    handled jar with wheel-engraved and gilt decoration, *182*, 183
    vase with applied decoration, 132, *133*
Spechter, 107
Spengler, W., 115
Spiller, Gottfried, 140
Spirit flask with wheel-engraved and enamel-painted decoration, 156, *157*
Stange, 107
Stangenglas, 120
Starr, Theodore, 199
Steuben Glass Works, 203, 211
Stevens and Williams Ltd., 199, 200, 211
Stiegel, Henry William, 184

Strabo, 44
Suetonius, 55
Sugar bowls
　of amber glass with mold-blown ribbing,
　　188, *189*
　of blown and tooled glass, covered, *186*, 187
　with furnace-worked decoration, covered,
　　190, 191
Sweden, 128, 219
Syria
　glassblowing in, 44
　glassmaking in, 13, 24, 43, 47, 63, 192
　lustred glass bowls, 76
　Mamluk enameled and gilt vase, 80, *81*
　mosque lamps, 83
　snake-thread glass in, 48

Table of colored glass mounted in ormolu,
　178, 179
Tamerlane (Timur), 80
Tazza, enameled, *102*, 103
Tel Asmar (Mesopotamia), 12
Tel Mahuz (Mesopotamia), 63, 67
T. G. Hawkes & Co., 203, 211
Thomas Webb and Sons, 199, 200
Thorpe, W. A., 60
Tiffany, Louis Comfort, 208, 212
Tiffany Glass and Decorating Company, 208
Tiffany Glass Company, 208, 212
Tree of Life (*homa*), 71, 72
Tumblers
　of enameled opaque white glass, 160, *161*
　wheel-engraved, and cover, 184, *185*
Tutankhamen (pharaoh),20
Tuthmosis III (pharoah), 19

Ulrika Eleonora (queen, Sweden), 128
United States
　Carder, Frederick, 211
　glassmaking in, 15, 184
　mold-blown pint flask, 192, *193*
　plaque carved in cameo technique, 200,
　　201
　pressed cake plate, *194*, 195
　sugar bowls, *186*, 187, 188, *189*, *190*, 191
　Tiffany, Louis C., 208, *209*

Van der Lith, Elisabeth, 152
Van Heemskerk, Willem, 131
Vases
　acid-etched, *214*, 215
　with applied decoration, 132, *133*
　cast and cut, *26*, 27
　with colored enclosures, *220*, 221
　cut glass, Sasanian, 64, *65*
　Daphne, 9, 47
　Egyptian, core-formed, *18*, 19
　"Favrile," with iridescent surface, 208,
　　209

"Intarsia," *210*, 211
Mamluk enameled and gilt, 80, *81*
with molded design, 212, *213*
red overlay, with wheel-engraved decora-
　tion, 180, *181*
two-handled, in dappled glass, 44, *45*
Veneziano, Agostino, 84
Venice (Italy), 14
　Chinese porcelain in, 87
　covered *cristallo* cup, *90*, 91
　cristallo, 107, 143
　diamond engraving in, 120, 123
　enameling in, 84, 103, 111
　glass-covered furniture, *178*, 179
　opaque white glass, 160
　paperweights, 196
Veronese, Paolo, 92
Verre de Nevers lampworked figure, *162*, 163
Verres à serpents, 124, *125*
Verzelini, Giacomo, 95
Verzelini glasses, 9, *94*, 95
Visscher, Anna Roemers, 131
Visscher, Maria Tesselschade Roemers,
　131
Von Eiff, Wilhelm, 216
Voronikhin, A. N., 179

Waldglas beaker, 88, *89*
Waldglas Roemers, 115
Wallander, Alf, 219
Warmbrunn (Silesia), 150
Waterpipes, *146*, 147
Wennerberg, G. G., 219
Wessler, Hans, 9, 135
Wheel-cut dish, *202*, 203
Wheel-engraved glass
　bowl, 52, *53*
　covered jar, 216, *217*
　crystal plaque, *134*, 135
　goblet, 136, *137*
　hookah base, *146*, 147
　portrait medallion, *174*, 175
　souvenir bottle, *54*, 55
　tumbler and cover, 184, *185*
Wheeler, Candace, 208
White Glass Works (U.S.), 188
Wineglasses, 92, *93*
　diamond-strippled, *154*, 155
　lattimo-threaded, 104, *105*
Winter, Friedrich, 139, 140, 150
Winter, Martin, 140
Wistar, Caspar, 184, 187
Woodall, Thomas and George, 200

Yung Chêng, 180

Zaffer, 167
Zanesville (U.S.), 188
Zuccarin, 100

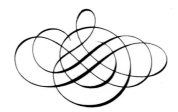